Ride the Wave

Ride the Wave

● ● ● ● ● ● ● ● ● ● ●

A Handbook for the Expatriate Family

BY *Monique Hammond*

Financial Consultant:
Tom Guglielmi CPA

**R. D. THOMAS
& Associates, Inc.**

Ride the Wave
A Handbook for the Expatriate Family
by Monique Hammond

This publication is designed to provide a clear straight-forward process for people considering expatriate assignments to evaluate: themselves, the assignment, their health, their finances and their family issues. It is also designed to provide some guidance through the process of preparing for, going on and returning from the assignment. It is sold with the understanding that the publisher is not engaged in rendering legal, accounting, psychological, health, fitness or financial service. If legal advice or other expert assistance is required, the services of a competent professional person should be sought. Examples cited in this book are for illustrative purposes only. All personal names and other identifying characteristics have been changed.

ISBN: 0-9663071-0-0
Library of Congress Catalog Card number: 98-090232

Published by R.D. Thomas & Assoc., Inc.
Minneapolis, Minnesota

Printed in the United States of America

Acknowledgements

One of my major challenges as an expat spouse was to keep myself motivated and energized. So when I started to write this book, I needed all the emotional support that I could get.

I want to thank ROSS HAMMOND, my husband, friend and teammate. Not only did he encourage me throughout the whole project but he also became my advisor, computer wizard and manager. Without his input, organizational skills and tireless efforts I might have never pulled the work together. I also want to thank our daughter HEIDI whose cheers of: "You are doing a great job, mom. Keep going!" were much needed music to my ears.

About the Author

Monique Hammond has lived and worked on 3 different continents. Monique was born and raised in Luxembourg City, Europe. She completed her pre-pharmacy training and worked as a pharmacist-intern in her native country. After moving to the United States, she graduated magna cum laude from the University of Minnesota College of Pharmacy. During her tenure as a hospital pharmacist, Monique's goal was to improve health care through community education and awareness. She wrote newspaper articles, did extensive public speaking and produced and hosted her own cable T.V. health show.

When the family was transferred to Australia, Monique continued to be active in community health education. She worked in the local public hospital and wrote a weekly newspaper column. Her efforts made her once more a popular speaker. During our stay, Monique also came into contact with other foreign families and found that many were inadequately prepared for life overseas. Drawing on her own experiences as well as on those of fellow expats, Monique wrote *Ride The Wave*, a handbook which provides prospective expatriate families with much needed information. Under the motto "Education Before Relocation," the book is a collection of personal feedback, vital questions and practical tips designed to guide the family through the 'big adventure.' After all, only a well-prepared expat is a happy and a productive expat.

Ross Hammond

TABLE OF CONTENTS

Introduction

What is An Expatriate?

An expatriate is anybody who lives outside of the homeland, or "Ex Patria," as the old Romans would have said. In times gone by, those who fell out of favor with their leaders or those who had committed certain crimes were chased from their country as a way of punishment.

Of course there are many reasons for leaving one's home, for becoming an expatriate. Missionaries traditionally tend to their flocks on foreign soil. Artists might go abroad in order to work in a more inspirational setting. Hopes for a better life and the quest for personal safety consistently convince people to leave the place of their ancestors behind and to relocate somewhere else.

In this book though, we shall talk about a special class of modern-day expatriates, whom we call "expats "for short. These people are given the opportunity to work for an employer on temporary assignments in a foreign land. They must clear the necessary immigration requirements but due to the limited duration of their stay they only enjoy limited privileges in the host country.

Even though it has exceptional status, the diplomatic service is probably the oldest kind of expat assignment. But what about average people such as managers, teachers, laborers, engineers? Can they become expats as well? As we move more and more towards a global economy, the network of companies with overseas ventures expands and so does the network of overseas foreign workers. Nowadays just about anybody can become the lucky winner of an expatriate tour.

Obviously, people who hate to travel, who are afraid of strangers, who loathe foreigners and who love to eat every meal with their two feet under their own kitchen table will make very bad expatriates. Those who dream of working a nine-to-five job from the safety of their own basements are also poor candidates. For such people overseas duty could become the nightmare of a lifetime. Globe-trotting is not for everybody!

Why Did I Write this Book?

Even though this book is aimed at the family as a whole, I would like to address the potential expat SPOUSE and parent. As the family manager and coordinator the spouse will become the cornerstone of the foreign mission. The decision to relocate demands big adjustments from every family member but especially from the spouse who usually tags along without a defined mission.

How should a spouse react when asked if he/she would like to join the partner for an expatriate tour ? Surprised? Shocked? Overjoyed? Even those whose initial enthusiasm cannot be bridled eventually will come back down to earth. To leave one's home, job, relatives and friends is a pretty revolutionary concept even for the bravest souls.

I gave up my job, close to 20 years of seniority with the company and my beloved pet projects, among others. When I boarded the plane, I did not quite know what to expect. I had given up the safety of my rut in order to venture into the big wide world. I trusted that a lot would be learned and gained from the very unique opportunity of living abroad. Yet, as many spouses have reported before me and as many will experience after me, I had a bit of trouble seeing the chance of a lifetime, particularly in the beginning.

First, I do not intend to sell you on an out-of-country tour if you feel that it is not right for you and your family. Expatriate duty is not for everybody. I met some people overseas who muddled through the motions but who would have been better off if they had turned the assignment down.

When I was first asked whether I would like to move to a different continent, I was rather overwhelmed. Initially, I saw nothing but obstacles. I felt mostly threatened by having to leave my comfortable routine that I had been in for years. Yet, the offer sounded intriguing to me, and eventually curiosity got the best of this cat!

As a family we did a lot of soul-searching, investigating and studying. I learned about the job and about our host country. In the end, I felt that we went into the adventure well-prepared! We certainly had done better than many of the other expats that I met along the way. But believe me, there were a lot of holes in my expat education. This is why I would like to share with you some of my own experiences as well as some of the surprises that greeted other unaware individuals.

Of course, it is impossible to be prepared for every situation that presents itself, but here is my motto:

A WELL-PREPARED EXPAT IS A
WELL-ADJUSTED, PRODUCTIVE AND HAPPY EXPAT.
Therefore: EDUCATION BEFORE RELOCATION!

This book is meant to help you make the decision whether expatriate duty is right for you and to prepare you for your impending assignment and move abroad. The big adventure starts long before the plane flies. There are loads of facts to be studied, work to be done and details to be taken care of. I sorted out my feedback from the trenches in the hope that it will help you deal with the dilemmas and with the wide range of emotions that are sure to overwhelm you as you figure out what is best for all involved. Keeping in mind that forewarned is forearmed, the goal of the book is to make you aware, right from the start, of the changes that lie ahead. It will also help you manage your expectations, fine-tune your feelings and cut down on the number of unwelcome surprises.

Nobody has problems handling success and the good times in life. Dealing with aggravations and with all sorts of unexpected events in a graceful fashion becomes a bit more challenging, especially if you are not on your own turf. An unaware expat is easily destabilized in the swells generated by the unforeseen. Overseas duty should be a time for reflecting, for learning and for growing. Read the book and you will not have to learn all over what those before you have learned already.

Another reason why I share some experiences is that no spouse should ever again waste precious moments feeling alone and worthless. This booklet is also meant to be an ego-booster for a major player in the expat experience: the spouse, mate or cohort of the working partner.

For the sake of discussion, I will assume that the expat couple is a married couple, hence the designation of 'spouse' for the accompanying partner. I am not an expert on legal rights and ramifications for accompanying partners of same-sex or unmarried couples. The challenge of dealing with all of the changes, both physical and emotional, that surround an overseas move is gargantuan for all people, regardless of marital status or gender.

A lot of thought and planning should take place before

one leaps into the turmoil that an overseas tour invariably will bring. As I already mentioned, I knew where I was going. I even expected to be struck by culture shock. I found out pretty soon that I was not as well prepared for the assignment as I thought I was. Was my situation unique? Absolutely not! Many of the expat spouses that I met overseas turned out to be just as bewildered as I was.

In order to shed some light on the financial challenges that surround expatriate relocation, Tom Guglielmi, CPA (certified public accountant) a friend and fellow expat kindly offered his feedback and thoughts. Can you afford to accept the overseas job? What about your pay, your taxes? The questions raised should at least point you in the right direction when you discuss your family situation with the experts in the field.

In the end, is an overseas assignment right for you? Only you can make that decision after you considered your own needs and situation as well as your family's circumstances. Every case is different. Hopefully, this handbook will put the joys and the concerns of expat life into perspective. It should give you some guidance on asking the not-so-obvious questions and teach you how take the good with the bad, how to deal with the ups and downs that expatriate life is famous for or how to RIDE THE WAVE. I included some of my home-made poems as humor breaks. Never underestimate the power of a solid sense of humor, particularly if you plan to become an expat.

Looking back at My Experience

Knowing what I know now, would I do it all over again? YES, I would. Even though living as an expatriate involved a move and plenty of adjustment, even though it tested my self-esteem and my sense of humor at times, it was worth every minute, every effort. It changed me and my outlook on the world, forever and hopefully for the better. At least I think that I became wiser, more tolerant and more self-assured in the process.

Finding joy even in unpleasant moments is a newly acquired skill that will hopefully stay with me for the rest of my life. My friend the laughing Kookaburra, this gorgeous bird and symbol of the Australian bush, taught me this when he would come and sit on the windowsill in search of company. His mere presence immediately dampened the impact of any daily crisis. How can one be sad or negative when there is such love and beauty?

Stepping back from life as-I-knew-it became a tremendous opportunity for self-discovery. The ability to do some thinking and reflecting cleared up a few misconceptions that I harbored in regard to my professional mission, for instance. Yes, I always loved my career as a hospital pharmacist, and I still do. But I did not necessarily love my on-line job. It gave me a lot of stress but often not much feeling of accomplishment. I did not realize this while I was still actively working. Too busy! No time to explore other options! If I ever return to the health system, I would like to do so as an educational resource.

I also found out that I love to write and that I have more talent for public speaking than I ever gave myself credit for. The different focus that expat duty put on life actually helped me redefine my dreams and my future goals. The invigorating breezes off the South Pacific ocean blew some cobwebs out of my brains that had entangled me in a rut to nowhere. Some surprise!

Fortunately overseas duty came at a good time for us. After some initial turmoil it turned into a once-in-a-lifetime opportunity that I would never surrender. True, at first it is somewhat bewildering to live in a different part of the globe. But life goes on, and eventually one picks up the rhythm and one learns how to negotiate the surf swells of expat life. One learns how to RIDE THE WAVE.

I

Will I Make a Good Expatriate?

What Is so Different about Expatriate Life?

Life is life, you say. No matter where you set up house, the routine remains the same: you cook, you clean, you shop for groceries, you worry, you rejoice. No matter where you are, life is not perfect. So what are some of the spices that give expatriate life such a distinct flavor?

Living overseas is both a challenge and a thrill. One might think of it as a total immersion program into a different community and culture. No amount of travel could have ever taught me in years what I learned in a few weeks of actually living abroad. Expatriate duty was not only a time for inner growth. It also exposed me to the various cultures in a portion of the world that I had never given much thought to. The benefits from such a horizon-expanding experience are beyond description. I, for one, will never be the same. But for all the good, there are also some less desirable features that have to be discussed.

- Physical and emotional distance from your home and support system introduce a certain vulnerability and instability into expat existence. You feel thrown outside of your comfort zone. Little problems easily become major dramas. You discover that you were more dependent on your entourage back home than you thought.

- Among rookie expats feelings of isolation and of lonesomeness tend to abound. The sudden realization that Fargo is far away also has something to do with acting like a fish out of water. But you'll settle in after a while. You will make new contacts among the other expats and among the local people. Life simply goes on. No worries!

- Since the assignment is temporary, you might start to look at life that way. Why invest time into making friends? You will leave anyway! Why consider the overseas address to be 'home'? Will it ever be home? An acquaintance once said that expatriate life is life in transition, a rent-a-life on someone else's turf. There may be some truth to that. It is best, however, to get rid of this type of wet-noodle attitude or it will keep you unsettled for the length of your stay. Relax! For the next few years home is where the frying pan is. Keep your eyes and ears open. Meet as many people as you can. Be like a sponge and soak up the experience.

- For the spouses lack of mission and purpose often lead to boredom and self-pity. It takes a lot of creative energy to carve a new, meaningful life for oneself. It takes patience and plenty of motivation to remain self-energized, day in and day out. But just think of all the things you always wanted to do but never had time for! Amaze yourself! Search and you will find your niche.

Expatriate life is different from being in the military service because a base offers a familiar social structure within which to function. There are still always people around who at least speak your language. There are stores with known products. Health and education services are provided. Even movie theaters and dry cleaning facilities are available. Everyday problems exist, but one tends to feel accepted and to find refuge in the microcosm of the military community.

When you are an expat you live and work in unfamiliar surroundings. The coddle-factor is zero. From one day to the next, you deal with different foods, different cultures and customs. You earn acceptance into the community. Often you might feel like a blind person finding your way in the dark. As an expat you are essentially on your own.

Why Are Expatriate Assignments Turned Down?

Windham International, together with the NFTC, (National Foreign Trade Council) found in their 1994 Global Relocation Trends Survey that, of the companies polled, 81% reported that all sorts of family related issues made candidates waver when offered an expat assignment or convinced them to turn it down. Why might a family be unwilling or unable to accept an expat assignment?

A) Types of family issues

• *Career conflicts and financial concerns*
The spouse cannot or will not relinquish his/her job or business. Maybe the family is not in a position to sacrifice the income that the spouse's job contributes. A 1992 Expatriate Dual Career Survey Report, sponsored by Windham International and NFTC, found that spouse career issues are frequently the reason why relocation offers are turned down. Some employers are taking notice and have started to offer expatriate spouse career programs.

• *Wrong timing!*
The family is unwilling to move because life at home is perfect. The dream house in the ideal location was just com-

pleted, and now is simply not a good time. For some families the timing will never be right because they are not interested in an overseas assignment, not now, not ever. The thought of an out-of-country tour instills sheer terror into some people.

• *Unexciting financial expat packages*
The incentives and the rewards offered are not commensurate with the sacrifices that the family would have to make. From a financial point of view the deal is not worth a major family upheaval.

• *Children who refuse to budge and torpedo the opportunity*

• *Academic considerations for kids*
Traditionally, it is a bad time to make major changes right around the last 2 years of high school. Faced with graduation and college concerns, many families often decide against relocating at this point.

• *Children with special needs*
Learning and physical disabilities as well as behavioral problems can often not be cared for properly overseas. Programs and facilities are either not available, too far way or substandard.

• *Aging parents who need care*

• *Health reasons of all kinds*

• *Administration of family business that cannot be managed long distance.*

B) **Problems with the location.**
In the 1994 Windham International/NFTC Global Relocation Trends Survey, 39% of companies reported that problems with the proposed location soured expat deals. (If the numbers do not seem to add up, it is due to the fact that the

respondents gave multiple answers as to why foreign assignments were refused.)

• *Climate*
The local climate might be incompatible with a family member's health. Intolerance to extreme heat, humidity or cold are often mentioned. Climate considerations are very individual and often are not subject to compromise.

• *Safety issues*
High crime rates, political strife and unrest at the proposed location are undesirable features. Who wants to spend months or even years in fear?

• *Cultural aspects that do not agree with the various family members*
Females might refuse to move to a place where women are second class citizens without rights or personal freedom.

• *Overall human rights practices that offend the family*

• *Third World countries or developing nations*
Assignments in these locations are often unattractive to families or even to single candidates because of general health, education, hygiene and safety concerns.

Why Do Expatriate Assignments Fail?

Failing assignments are expensive both for the family and for the company. Expats are high-risk, high-cost investments. Lowering the failure rate is one of the great challenges facing those in international business. An assignment obviously fails if the expat cannot handle the job or if the expat returns home before the contract is up. It can be hard to determine the exact reasons for such failures because often the 'real' causes do not come to the attention of those in charge.

A) Family problems!

In their June 1996 issue, *Personnel Journal* reports that 45% of the organizations responding to their survey had expatriate families return home early, leaving the assignee behind on the job. Even if the working partner stays on site, it can be assumed that the split of the family will interfere with his/her professional concentration.

• *Illness*
Illness due to intolerance of climate, aggravation of an existing condition, job related stress or contracting a sickness native to the new land can convince expatriates that the time has come to head home.

• *Children*
Extreme homesickness, failure to fit in, illness, refusal to stay or even trouble with the law might be some of the reasons why a family has to terminate an assignment.

• *Problems with kids' education*
Schools are substandard or otherwise unacceptable. Companies may offer to pay the tuition for private or boarding schools in an effort to save the project.

• *Relationship trouble*
Stress due to relocation can do funny things to people. If there is a major breakdown in the expat couple's relationship due to a lack of communication, conflicting interests or even affairs, the handwriting is obviously on the wall.

• *Failure to cope*
Again, extreme homesickness and general unhappiness can seriously compromise the family well-being and thus the project. Tensions within the family unit greatly decrease the effectiveness of the working partner. Too many distractions!

B) Problems with the location

After the big move the family might come to the conclusion that the location is indeed totally unacceptable to them. They will not stay. Period.

C) Problems at the job

• *Inability to handle the job*

Once on site, the candidate fails at the job. Goals and expectations are not met. Often personality and/or management style get in the way. The inability to think 'globally' often becomes the downfall for managers.

• *Getting on the wrong side of the local population*

The candidate fails to function within the cultural setting. The head office does not appreciate reports of clashes at the business site or accounts of barroom brawls involving their employees. Strained relationships with local people, trade unions or business partners create an unhealthy business climate and can terminate assignments in a hurry.

• *Lack of integrity*

Exercising bad judgement when it comes to relationships with other employees, serious mismanagement of company money, travel and expense account abuses make the bosses at home question the expat's reliability and honesty. The problem is often solved with a one-way ticket home.

The great personal and financial losses derived from failed expatriate missions have convinced some companies to try various techniques in order to curb the failure rate. Besides using more careful screening guidelines, employers also have come to recognize the absolute necessity of better training programs. It is no longer a secret that sending unprepared expat candidates and their families abroad is a setup for failure.

Ferreting out the ideal candidates is only part of the company's task. How to keep the expat and the family happy and efficient while they are on location and how to repatriate them without major trauma are problems that have to be addressed.

In March 1995, *Training* magazine published an article by John R. Engen on the problems of repatriation. An interesting finding was that some companies have put in place mentoring programs which assign the expat to a contact in the home office. This home-site sponsor keeps in touch with the overseas employee, informs him/her of the happenings in the company and serves as a liaison person when the expat returns home once the contract is up.

There could be an added bonus to such a program: as the assignment progresses the sponsor might detect job or family problems that can be addressed before major damage is done.

When Do Expatriate Assignments Succeed?

Assignments succeed when there is a happy match between the job, the candidate and his/her family. The employee is able to handle the job and can make the expected business goals. The family sees the opportunity for both professional and personal growth, has a positive attitude and is willing to relocate and to work as a team. Things look even better if the timing of the offer is right.

For successful missions the decision to take on the challenge must be based on sound facts rather than on grandiose expectations, illusions or even paranoid anxieties. (see chapter on 'testing of motives')

Some Basic Questions at the Start

I found that the most crucial portion of the whole adventure started long before we actually left. It began with the telephone call that introduced the possibility of an overseas assignment into our lives. Once you receive that guess-what call, your mind will be boggled by a multitude of questions. Let's look at some of the most obvious and most crucial ones:

- *Are you willing to consider a move?*

At first I was not too excited mostly because I was taken by surprise. It all sounded so tedious and drastic! Yet, a little taste for adventure made me say that I would give the proposal some serious thought. Even before I hung up, I knew that it would be worth taking a risk in order to have the very unique experience of living overseas.

Moving becomes a key issue if you happen to live in your dream house, in the ideal location for you. Chances are that you do not want to abandon your homestead, the social circuit or the fabulous school system for a somewhat adventurous, uncertain future.

I knew a spouse who found herself in that dilemma. She was happy where she was, and she had no intention of going anywhere else. Travel was both boring and threatening to her, and so she tried the old compromise trick: she showed up for a few weeks at her husband's overseas location after which she promptly headed home for another 3 months. The arrangement turned out to be very disruptive, expensive, unfulfilling and unsatisfactory. Needless to say her husband found no support in her, and her continuously changing travel plans caused plenty of confusion. The adventure came to an end after less than a year. One cannot live on both sides of the street. One either makes a commitment or one does not.

- *Are you independent enough to function on your own without your support system of family, friends and acquaintances at close range?*

While overseas, Linda's husband wished that he had encouraged his wife to think a bit more on her own. He 'took care' of Linda, and her assignment was to please her man. And so she followed him on expatriate tour. This totally dependent woman became almost suicidal when she was thrown out of her cocoon, with family and friends unreachable for emergency counsel. Linda was now a resentful burden to her husband and the social project of the other expat spouses.

Expatriates have to be somewhat creative not only in daily life but especially when it comes to solving problems and to approaching possible crisis situations. People who need the continuous approval of others before they can make a decision, who panic easily and who have to discuss every minute detail of their lives with a confidant should do some serious soul-searching. Time differences often make it difficult to contact people at home at a moment's notice. Companies usually do not offer a 1-800-don't-panic number, even though this would be a great idea. Being self-reliant is a definite plus if you contemplate expat life. It will help you make the adjustment to the new location a lot faster, and it will also ease homesickness attacks.

- *Do you know where you are relocating to?*

Real estate people keep telling us that there are 3 reasons why clients buy a particular home: location, location and location. Of course, you can see yourself in one of the great capitals of the world, shopping and sipping espresso in an outdoor Café on a 'grand boulevard.' Glamorous power-assignments do exist, especially in the financial, banking or high-level management sectors. But if you talk about mining, oil drilling, power production and the like, count on a location a bit further out of town.

I was told of a lady who thought that she would move to Jakarta. She had visited there before and felt that she could cope with the location. Then she found out that the plane just landed there. Her husband's actual assignment was about 200 miles outside of the city. She was a little shaken by the discovery, but she rode the wave to perfection and became a specialist in jungle living in no time at all. One can never ask too many questions!

If you are a big-city person, would you consider living in a small town where everybody knows everybody? If you come from a small town, will the crowds in the city drive you bonkers? Think about it!

Ever since I was a child, I knew that I never wanted to live in a village or 'in the country' as one might say. Isolation, muddy roads and certain smells get to me. I certainly did not need a metropolis to make me happy, but I wanted to be in a town of some sort. I have simply never been a backpacker or a country girl.

There are plenty of people who react exactly in the opposite way of how I reacted. They hate cities and towns. They love roughing it. To each his/her own! Only you know what the minimum requirements are that make a place livable for you. Ponder your options but most of all ask questions and pinpoint the exact place where you will be. This could eliminate some nasty surprises.

• *How long will your assignment be?*
Assignments that are open-ended or that are too long tend to breed resentment after a while. People suddenly feel trapped because they can't detect any light at the end of the tunnel.

From those of us who have been there, two to three years should do it. The longer you are away, the harder it will be to reintegrate back into your own society, to keep friendships going or to keep a foot in the door with an employer. Professional networks also tend to disintegrate with time.

After a while, no matter how well you are adjusted, some feelings of isolation and of homesickness will probably gnaw at you. You will also notice that the old desire to achieve some of your own goals is still alive. Especially spouses who used to have their own careers report that they got kind of restless because they wanted to carry on with their lives. Incidentally, working partners who love their overseas jobs and who truly enjoy living abroad can be tempted to extend the length of their contracts. Therefore it is all the more important for the spouse to know exactly how long the assignment will be. If the decision is made to stay longer than the original agreement, you should have your say before further commitments are made.

The length of stay also determines what happens to your house, your cars and the rest of your possessions. For a short while a house can be rented out or a family member or friend might be able to house-sit for you. Years and years of absence, however, usually dictate the sale of the homestead.

Some expatriates do not want to return to life as they knew it. They become rather fascinated by this globe-trotting existence and volunteer for more assignments. Those who became such 'professional' expats recommend to keep tours of duty back-to-back. Moving home and then out again is disruptive and not recommended by those who have done it.

• *Are you willing to put your own career and dreams on hold?* Will you, the spouse, be able to work in your profession? Can you strike up a deal with your employer such as taking a temporary leave from your present job? Can your projects wait until you get back? Can you continue to work on your special projects while you are overseas? It is quite possible to do so, as I found out. How driven are you? How much do you actually love what you are doing now? Will you feel totally decimated if you have to switch tempo and style for a while? Maybe this time 'away from it all' will give you the chance to perfect or to pursue some new task that the distractions in your present life keep you from concentrating on. There could be some opportunities of a different kind ahead!

When it comes to expat assignments, spouses with solid careers or businesses of their own are a company's nightmare. As I mentioned already, the spouse not being able or willing to surrender a well-paying job or business venture are major reasons why expat assignments are turned down. However, visa restrictions, difficulties in getting work permits, language barriers, labor laws, licensing requirements and tax complications among others often do not allow the spouse to work for pay in the new land. In spite of these technical difficulties, there are an amazing amount of spouses who welcome the change that overseas duty brings. Once settled in their new homes, they often volunteer their services for the benefit of the local communities.

I think of Janice, the ballerina, who closed the door on her ballet school in a fashionable suburb when her husband was transferred. They relocated to a small town in Central Queensland where she truly enjoyed teaching the local children her graceful art. She gave them an opportunity that they would have never had otherwise.

Then there was Mel, the college professor, who became an expat when his wife was sent on overseas duty. He learned a lot of new things in a new place while he taught in a local literacy program.

- *Do you have a 'portable' career?*

Consultants, reporters, writers, poets, seamstresses and other lucky folk are not tied to an office building in order to work the magic of their trades. Computers, fax machines and E-mail make it easier nowadays to keep in touch with possible assignments in the homeland. Unfortunately, some careers simply do not have the luxury of flexibility built into them.

If you, the spouse, are able to work for pay while overseas, clarify your tax situation and compensation arrangements ahead of time. Make sure that it will not actually cost you money to work. I know of a few cases where the spouses quit their for-pay activities because of very unfavorable tax consequences.

Profile of the Ideal Expatriate Candidate

First, consider being picked for overseas duty as a great compliment from your company. It is a vote of confidence that should at least flatter the candidate and his/her family. Not everybody is considered for this honor. Companies invest a lot of money in order to secure the services and the expertise of the person targeted for an expatriate position. They are not too keen on sending exact replicas of the proverbial 'Ugly American' to represent their interests. They need a kinder, gentler type of person who is competent and charismatic but who can be tough as nails should the need arise.

So why were you singled out? Why was your partner picked? Probably because he/she fits the profile of the ideal expatriate employee.

To do overseas duty the candidate should

- have a high degree of expertise in his/her field,
- be respectful of the culture and people of the host country,

- exhibit at least some enthusiasm for the assignment,
- be healthy and fit,
- be able to shoulder responsibility,
- have leadership potential,
- make decisions independently,
- handle stress well,
- have a great sense of humor,
- be loyal to the company,
- be sensitive to the needs and feelings of others,
- be a good diplomat and take care of business all at once.

Then we have the bonus points. These extra features make an employee all the more attractive for an overseas transfer.

He/she

- is already familiar with the country in question, (stationed there with military or extensive travel)
- speaks the language,
- has a particular love or fascination for the country,
- loves to travel,
- loves to meet people of different cultures and backgrounds,
- has a sense for adventure,
- if married, the spouse and family share the views and the feelings of the individual about moving out-of-country,
- is single or divorced.

Being single or divorced is often viewed by companies as a positive point. It is considered to be cheaper and less complicated to send an unattached person on expat duty rather than somebody who will take along all those appendages called a family. Especially with the problems caused by dual career couples and by kids, picking the single guy might make a lot of sense. Due to the headaches that family concerns bring, human resource people are often tempted to give preference to an unattached candidate even though he/she might actually not be the best choice for the job.

Such decisions obviously bring on trouble of a different kind. Let's look at the divorced employee for instance. Legal and personal problems do not disappear simply because the candidate goes overseas. In a way, it will be more costly and stressful to manage the situation from a distance. Divorced candidates should check out ahead of time what such an out-of-country move means to them in legal terms. Are there any problems in regard to alimony obligations? How will the move affect child custody and visitation rights?

It is also known that single and otherwise unattached expats tend to be hit harder by feelings of isolation and lonesomeness. Single males are often sent on so-called Rambo assignments. These are posts that are too isolated, too primitive or too dangerous and off-limits to families. Being stranded without any kind of personal support system is more than some people can take.

An Important Link in the Expatriate Chain: The Spouse

Expatriate couples work as a TEAM. A team is made up of at least two people. In the expatriate situation the spouse is definitely a team member. So how come that spouses often feel taken for granted and ignored by company officials?

Is it true that employers tend to grossly underestimate the spouse's role in the expatriate experience? This could be a very costly mistake!

As companies embark on complicated, expensive foreign ventures, it is easy for them to become all wrapped-up in business issues and to forget about people issues. As we shall see, expatriate spouses are intimately associated with company business, yet they seem to be frequently undervalued.

Quite a few expatriate spouses to whom I have talked voiced their disappointment that nobody in the home office seemed to care much about their opinion. No matter how frequently they went 'home,' they were never invited to talk to expat liaison people about their overseas experience. Most of these spouses had been professionals in their own right back home. Of course it was unsettling to them that feedback from their side of the trenches did not figure highly on the agenda of those in charge. The working partners were routinely grilled on the business aspects of the experience while the human perspective ended up on the back burner.

One lady stated that she made a list of concerns so that her husband could present these when meeting with human resource representatives back in the homeland. Did anybody ever contact her personally to find out more? No! Their loss! The company could have learned plenty from this lady's suggestions. Their future expats will have to go through the same trauma that their predecessor went through, learning everything all over again!

The feeling that their task was accomplished once they had signed on the dotted line has left plenty of spouses quite frustrated. Were they the least bit important to the company? What exactly was their mission? They were left with the impression that they had their time in the limelight with the expat liaison person before their departure. They had agreed to accompany their partners. As far as the company was concerned, they had been briefed, and they served their purpose. All they had to do now was to embark quietly on the slow, leaky boat to China, without any particular role, minding their Ps and Qs.

The important lesson to learn is that, even though the company depends on you to help turn a mission into a success, you should never depend on them to boost your feelings of self-worth or to define a mission for you. Take your cues from your partner and from the situation that presents itself once you arrive on site. Find your niche. Define your own mission and just do it!

The expat spouse might not figure on the payroll, but he/she is the co-ambassador for the company and for the native country. Most of all, the spouse is the support system upon which the partner relies no matter what the situation. Without a dependable SUPPORT SYSTEM the 'adventure' can easily turn into a very stressful, lonesome experience. The spouse is often the only person who can be totally trusted by the partner when it comes to discussing personal problems and maybe sensitive personnel or business issues.

Suffice it to say that you should never doubt your own importance while on expat mission. Your partner needs a sounding board, a confidant with whom he/she can brainstorm and whose discretion is one-hundred percent guaranteed.

But weren't you always your partner's best friend, his/her travel companion and sometimes comic relief, even before the start of this whole adventure thing? Of course, but then there were all those other pals and business associates around with whom your partner could consult and communicate. As expatriates, there are often just the two of you.

My husband told me now and then that without me he could not have handled his job. "You earn half of my salary," he said on a dark day when I had a major worthlessness attack. Do you know what? The man spoke the truth! It took me the better part of a year to realize that he did not just try to pacify me. MUCH OF HIS BUSINESS SUCCESS DEPENDED ALSO ON MY PERFORMANCE! I was active in the community, accompanied him to official functions and hosted business partners and visiting company officials. I also kept in contact with the spouses of fellow expats and business partners. Anyway, I earned my keep!

Let me tell you about Sally. She lived in an expat situation without ever learning a great deal about the area or about the country where she spent a considerable amount of time. She never had a lot of interests. She never had much of an opinion about anything, and, if she did, nobody ever heard it.

Sally should fit the profile of the ideal expat wife: compliant, patient, almost lifeless, no bother, no problem. Far from it! She was a bit of an albatross around her husband's neck. He had very little support and help from Sally. She could have cared less about the community that she lived in. She never invited her husband's colleagues or business partners for a picnic. He never had to look her way in order to get his rundown batteries recharged with loads of encouragement. Sally simply was no spark plug. Her husband was glad when his tour of duty came to an early end.

By now it should be clear to you that, as an expat spouse, you have a big job to do. Agreed! It will sometimes become tiring and frustrating to be continuously self-motivating. Yet, even without feedback from the head-office, never forget that in the expat scenario you are an asset to your partner and thus to the company. A spouse can make or break an assignment as we have seen. So be assured that your role is a vital one. You are not just extra baggage. You are indeed a most important link in the expatriate experience.

What are some spouse requirements and qualifications for successful overseas duty? Many of the points already mentioned for the partner also apply to the expatriate spouse. Ideally, he/she:

- has a positive attitude,
- has a solid sense of humor and an endless string of patience,
- likes to travel, to meet people of different cultures,

- is able to remain diplomatic no matter what the situation,
- knows the importance of discretion and confidentiality,
- has a sense of adventure,
- is able to cope with radical changes in rapid succession, is 'flexible,'
- is willing to give up own career or surrender own business,
- is independent, creative and self-reliant,
- is not an emotional burden for everybody involved,
- has some fun and is some fun,
- looks upon the assignment as an opportunity to learn and to grow, not as a prison sentence,
- prefers being active to being bored,
- accepts that the partner basks in the limelight.

The higher the position, the more truth there is to the last statement. Will your ego allow you to play second fiddle? Think about it! Is it within you to exchange your feelings of jealousy for feelings of pride? Anybody who has a problem with selfless behavior will get a crash course in a hurry.

Overall, a competent, friendly, fun, flexible, patient, positive, pleasant, selfless, self-confident, tactful, interested person will do as an expat spouse. Obviously, no common mortal possesses all of the above qualities. We all have our shortcomings.

But, a positive attitude, patience and a good sense of humor should definitely be part of your expat-personality-survival-kit. They always save the day. So don't leave home without them!

A Word about 'Split' Assignments

The fact that you are given a chance to accompany your partner is extremely good news. You could have been offered the 'splits.' Some assignments can be so nasty and dangerous that on-site family involvement is not even considered. Then you are faced with a "now-you-see-me, now-you-don't" situation where long periods of separation and of erratic visiting schedules test the patience of even the most complacent of spouses. For most people the 'splits' are the pits!

Let me give you an example of what I mean by the splits.

For safety reasons, many expat families of Papua New Guinea (PNG) oil field and mine workers live along the east coast of Queensland, Australia. I have been told that, since PNG has its political problems, workers often perform their duties under the watchful eyes of armed guards. On-site employees live in compounds similar to army bases. They work for periods of up to four weeks at a time after which they join their loved ones in Australia for a visit of about two weeks. You can guess that the time spent together better be quality time or there will be some problems pretty fast. In my opinion, this is a rough arrangement.

Will the family survive such tests of worries, separation and stress ? Are split assignments worth the gamble? It is a tough call. This is the time when you really have to consider your options and your priorities. Personally, I would never take even the remote chance of jeopardizing our marriage. No matter how close a couple is, once distance and time come between two people, focus is inevitably lost. Part-time relationships simply do not do it for me. What is gained if one ends up on the casualty roster?

Of course, there are people who do not like each other that well and who might welcome some time apart. To each his own.

Frequently, financial considerations tip the balance in favor of split tours of duty. Hopefully, the stint is short, the career opportunity exceptional and the reward good, or should we say outstanding.

Considering all of the above frustrations, aren't you lucky that you and the kids can go along with your partner? Isn't it great that you can all live together and share this once-in-a-lifetime adventure?

Your Relationship with Your Partner:
Trust Is a Must

In order to accomplish the tasks demanded of an expatriate couple, a solid relationship between the partners is a must. If this is not the case, the stresses of an overseas assignment will be testing the family ties to the breaking point. Expatriate life forces you to operate a lot outside of your comfort zone and thus will tear a shallow partnership to shreds. Marital discord is hard enough to cope with on the home turf. Don't fool yourself by hoping that a change of pace or a change of scenery might do your rocky union some good. It's conceivable but highly unlikely.

Opportunities for infidelity exist anywhere in the world, but expat assignments do carry some extra risks. Prostitutes working the lobbies of hotels famous for housing overseas workers are certainly not an unusual sight. Now and then it might also become difficult to resist pampering and accommodating office staff that endeavor to ease an expat's feelings of lonesomeness or to tickle his or her ego. Finding out that your partner plays the field is always distressing. Finding out while you are in a foreign land is a disaster.

A marriage already marred by bouts of infidelity and by miscellaneous breaches of trust is also not the type to withstand the sometimes rigorous demands and temptations of expat life. Being absolutely assured of each other's love and support is probably the single most important ingredient for pulling off a successful overseas tour of duty. If you present a united front, there will be very few challenges that you cannot handle. Remember that you are a team!

Before accepting a transfer to Ulan Bator in Mongolia, take some time to reflect on the relationship that exists between the two of you. Many people live together for years and never even realize that they cannot communicate with each other. They simply share space. She consults her mother or her friend Mandy when there is a problem. He calls on his buddy Fred when life comes crashing down on him.

With family and friends far away, expatriate couples are forced to focus more on each other. Increased togetherness can become a problem for those people who are not best friends. Who is your most valued ally in the jungles of Java? Hopefully the person sitting next to you under the breakfast palm—your partner.

Living abroad introduces a certain amount of vulnerability into lives, especially into spouses' lives. Usually spouses become financially dependent on the partner who holds the working visa and who earns the pay. It takes a lot of trust to be 'dependent' on someone, especially if you are used to making your own money and if you enjoyed your independence. This is a major mental hurdle that has to be overcome. Does your partner have the heart and the patience that it takes in order to help you bridge this gap? Now is a good time to evaluate how much faith you actually have in each other.

In life there are never any guarantees. Yet, in expat situations plenty of surprises will certainly be part of the deal. Children may go berserk, teenagers can fall hopelessly in love, illness might hit, a partner could be sexually harassed. Of course, none of the above events are unique to overseas life, but once you are oceans apart from family and friends, problems are magnified by a factor of at least ten.

Ideally, adversity should draw the family together. Often this is not the case due to a lack of loyalty, love and trust between the various members right from the start. If you feel that there are cracks in your relationship that need patching, do not wait. See a counselor before you leave or before you even consider the assignment. Your whole future could be at risk. IF YOU FAIL AS A COUPLE, YOU—THE SPOUSE—HAVE THE MOST TO LOSE. When the house of cards comes tumbling down, you face a breakup in a foreign country with little or no support and few choices. Sure, you can always go home and put your life back together, but it will be tough. Remember: you quit your job, you probably sold your house, your car. What about the children and long distance legal battles? Things start to look pretty grim.

For your own sake, give yourself a chance. Make sure that your partnership has a clean bill of health before the start of the big adventure. It's not nice to get dumped somewhere in the desert after the last camel heading back to civilization has left.

HUMOR BREAK
THE CALL TO ADVENTURE

"Good afternoon, honey, this is your Ross.
I got wonderful news today from the boss!
I am on the list for an expat tour now.
How about four years in lovely Macao?
Or would you like Bali, Australia, Gabon?
Your wish's my command. I'll sign us right on.
It's an honor to be asked for such duty, I hear.
The chance of a lifetime is ever so near:

To ride the wave of life's raging, wild surf,
to get away for a bit from the old home turf!"

"Four years is for ever. Can I take the cat?
And what by the way is such an expat?"

"An expat's a gypsy, an adventurer of sorts
who works for his company in far away ports.
Expats for companies are a tad hard to get.
Come on, why aren't you excited just yet?
Think over the offer for the boss wants to know
when we'll say yes, when we will go."

"I think about the house, the kids and my job.
What about grandma and old cousin Bob?"

"It wouldn't be as bad as it might now seem,
but we must endeavor to work as a team.
Four years will fly by in no time at all.
We'll visit already here early next Fall."

"To tell you the truth, my old rut is a bore.
It lacks challenge, future, excitement and more.
I'll come to your office tomorrow at eight.
Let's sign for Australia before it's too late.
Wouldn't you love to see Sydney and a wild kangaroo,
the Great Barrier Reef, Melbourne and Uluru?
Bob will house-sit for he likes the view.
Besides, it will give him something to do.
And now let's hope that the kids will behave
so that together we can all ride that wave."

II

Do I Want this Assignment at this Time?

Your Name is on the List: A Setup for Change

Usually, the whole sequence of events starts with a telephone call, preferably right around suppertime as you attempt to adjust the spices for the meatloaf: "Guess what! I was put on the list for this job in Timbuktu."

This is the beginning of a major change in your life. Whether you are stunned or overly excited, keep an open mind. Most importantly, don't panic! You are not on that plane yet! The wheels of a lengthy selection process are barely turning. But then again, there are always exceptions!

Some people are 'chosen' for overseas duty without a lot of hassle. They might have a 'sponsor' high enough on the seniority ladder of the company who simply sends them abroad as a favor. Not going through the interviewing process can be a drawback for the candidate and for the company. The prospective expat is probably sent on his/her merry way uninformed and unprepared. It is simply not a given that a productive and effective worker in one particular setting functions equally well in an out-of-country situation. Some 'favors' can turn into disasters.

The name of an acquaintance comes to mind whose depressing expatriate experience ended his career with the company after many years of service. Let's call him Greg. Greg had been sent by a buddy who 'pulled some strings' on overseas tour. Even though he had a good mind for business and was a decent manager back home, Greg never succeeded in thinking globally. He tried to lay down rules in the work place that were not compatible with the local culture. He crossed the union leaders and did not satisfy the home office's demands for financial results. Greg's reward turned into his demise.

The more responsibility the expat assignment carries, the higher the position, the more the candidate is, and should be, scrutinized. For lofty management jobs the partner will probably be put through what seems like endless interviews, applications and even psychological profiles. Suddenly expertise, willingness to relocate and promises to honor a contract are not qualifications enough. Then what do we expect? An expat is a high-buck investment, and the employers want to make darn sure that they got the right person for the job.

After the interviews come the fretting and the waiting. This can be a stressful time for all concerned. How soon will a company include the whole family in the process? That depends. The more candidates there are, the longer they will probably wait. Before upsetting the apple cart, they want to make certain that there is a reasonable possibility that your partner will be the 'chosen one.' So until a decision is made, spouses are often left on the outside of the process.

Remember that the adventure starts long before the plane ride! Do not let yourself be thrown out of the loop! The time to prepare yourself for an impending major change is now. It will take a while to just familiarize yourself with the idea of living in a foreign country.

As soon as the possibility arises that you and your family

might be transferred overseas, your life will change. Your status quo, well organized lifestyle will change. Once companies consider employees for major moves such as overseas assignments, the issue will resurface. We live in a global economy and in today's business world an expatriate tour of duty becomes a distinct possibility for workers of all levels. Test yourself: if you are not interested right now in relocating, will you be interested at some point in the future? Be honest with the company. You might not be chosen this time around to move to Tierra del Fuego, but your name is on the list. Change is in the air, now or later.

Next, do some homework. Getting actively involved gives you a feeling of taking control of the situation. Later on, if you are picked for the assignment, you will be ready to discuss the whole matter in an intelligent and coherent fashion. Research your project and familiarize yourself with your prospective new home. The exercise will help you work through the mental process that is so important when it comes to dealing with change. You will also accumulate the information necessary to help you decide whether you would make a good expat at the proposed location.

The Decision Making Process—Questions to Ask Yourself

Career conflicts and family matters emerge as serious stumbling blocks when decisions about overseas relocation are made. As we have seen, they are often cited as reasons why assignments are turned down and why they fail. Based upon the knowledge of their circumstances, most people have some sort of gut feeling about the offer right from the start. Besides the obvious question of job qualifications, there will be eventually three major factors that determine whether an expat assignment is right for all involved: family issues, financial concerns and health matters.

Since overly inflated expectations and being felled by un-welcome surprises are the biggest reasons why expats do not have a good time once they are on site, thorough preparation is the key to effective expectation and surprise management. Only an informed decision will be a good decision when faced with the prospect of expatriate duty.

1) Are you at all interested in a move?
What was your initial reaction to the news of a potential re-location? Check on your attitude. If you feel that there is no way that you will ever pack up and move out-of-country, then you got your answer already. Communicate your feel-ings to your partner and to the company.

After I got over the initial shock, I felt that my level of in-terest was in the definite-maybe range. I simply needed loads of more specific information before I could make up my mind.

2) Ask your partner how he/she feels about the job. What does he/she know about the job? (See checklist)
Before you get all upset and turn the family upside-down, try to assess if you are dealing with a feasible proposal. Is your partner qualified for the job? How does he/she feel about the responsibilities and duties that the job will bring? Is your partner interested in the job in the first place? Are you deal-ing with a new venture or with an established situation? Un-less you are sent to fix a messy state of affairs, it is usually more stressful and demanding to set up a brand-new busi-ness than it is to take over one that is already on a steady course. Who will be in charge of the project? How does the partner feel about reporting to this person?

How long will your assignment be? I mentioned this al-ready. If the assignment seems too long, can you bargain on that issue?

Learn as much as possible about the business details of the job itself. After all, the job draws the relocation.

Once you get past these basics, discuss the situation with your partner and children. Play the 'what-if' game and get everybody's feelings and feedback. Writing down every thought and concern will help you later on when you weigh the pros and the cons of the mission.

3) *Is the timing of the offer right?*

Even though I was somewhat startled when I got the guess-what telephone call, the assignment offer came at a very opportune moment for us. After five years in his job, my husband felt like diving into a new project. I had started to refocus my efforts within my profession, and even our daughter wanted to change schools. For us, the timing was right.

Maybe you are not as fortunate. Maybe the kids' education, your career or relatives who need to be cared for are only some of the reasons that forbid you at present to become expats. Again, would you consider to keep your options open for a future assignment? Now might be the moment to level with your partner and with the company on the subject.

4) *Do you know enough about the host country in order to form a rational opinion?*

• Where exactly are Estonia, Queensland or Java? Will you go to Mali or to Bali? I certainly had to sharpen my geography skills before I could form any kind of an opinion on our expatriate assignment.

Travel with the finger on the map. Start to gather some relevant information. Cruise into Cyberspace or simply get some books and some travel magazines on the subject. Call the embassy or the local consulate for reference material on your potential host country's history, laws, economy, language and people. Look at the country from the point of view of somebody who will live there.

- Now is as good a time as any to establish your own list of 'Must-Haves' for quality of life. You will probably notice—as I did—that you will become more flexible, more ready to compromise on some of the issues that you first perceive as being absolutely vital for survival and happiness. In the process of studying up on your host country you gain new insight and understanding that might swing your opinion somewhat.

In the back of the book I compiled a list of commonly mentioned 'Must-Haves.' You can put together your own list. Be sure though that you come up with exactly 15 items otherwise you throw off the scoring chart. Eventually the last exercise will be to determine if your newly acquired knowledge has changed your attitude at all towards your original 'Must-Haves' or absolutes.

My first reaction to life in a small town was quite negative. Then I found out while doing my homework that our particular town was a harbor town which rated highly with me. It was also very well equipped with a modern shopping center, a library, a theater and so on. To that I added the beneficial effects from decreased stress, noise and traffic levels. Bingo! My initial −5 rating for small town life turned into a +6. By the time we left our host town, city life scored a −8 with me. One should really never say never!

During my studies I also found out that I did not need the latest electrical gadgets, designer clothes or foods processed according to the latest fads in order to be happy. But worries about hygiene, disease and food and water safety rated very highly on my charts. I do not expect life to be perfect, but I do know what stresses me to the max. This is why I absolutely did not want to go a Third World country. There is nothing wrong with such an assignment for the right person.

I simply was not the right person. When the opportunity presented itself, I counted myself out.

So, do your research and get ready for some surprises. Learning about a place is never a waste of time. It might just stimulate your interest and let you see the potential of the proposed assignment or it might validate your anxieties. One thing is for sure: you will learn a lot about the area in question and more about yourself. In the end, those people who are the least prepared are also the ones who are the least happy once they are overseas.

Gerry took the attitude of "I'll find out soon enough what this place is like," and never bothered to read up on Saudi Arabia. The company put her through some material, but Gerry acted like the proverbial ostrich and stuck her head in the sand. Later on she admitted that she could have saved herself a lot of turmoil by being more involved right from the start.

• What is the political situation in your host country?

How many religious factions are fighting each other? Is the place under unstable military rule? Are there other foreign companies in the area or will you be the only expats? Sometimes there can be safety in numbers. Compromising personal safety is sheer craziness. The best business opportunities might be in such areas where rules are few and where real estate and labor are cheap. But that does not mean that such places offer a lot of secure choices when it comes to relocating a family.

• What do you know about the climate in your prospective new home?

Never underestimate the weather issues! Will all members of the family be able to tolerate the climate? High humidity is often cited as the most unpleasant weather factor.

• What do you know about the school system in your host country?

In our group the school issue turned out to be a major concern and problem for those people who took the children along. Will the kids' education be adequate? Will they be able to make the transition back into the system of their homeland without major trauma? See the chapter on "Site Visit" for some questions and concerns regarding education.

• If you are female, what is the status of women in your potential new home?

• How are people of your race or nationality treated in your host country?

• How does the local society view foreigners in general?

I am not advocating that one run away from life, but is it really worth the aggravation and maybe the danger that come from bucking a system? One can get slashed tires and trashed yards anywhere. When one is thousands of miles from home however, hostility takes on a totally new meaning. Remember that it is important to come out of the experience alive and still somewhat mentally balanced.

• Is there a church of your denomination available at your new location?

Before jumping into the big adventure, it is extremely important to get into the clear on religious issues. How religious are you? Are you very specific in your religious beliefs? How strong are the ties to your current church? Do your religious convictions enter into conflict with human rights practices in your prospective new home?

Expats often find that a church of their denomination does not exist at their location. In some small towns in Australia it was not unusual for Catholics and Anglicans (Episcopals) to share the same premises. Services were often held together. Expats might find themselves in a M*A*S*H-type situation where one Father Mulcahy serves all faiths. It all comes down to how flexible you are in religious matters. Investigate the situation. Maybe expat life at the proposed location is not for you.

• Is there anybody who can give you a firsthand account of what it is like to live in your assigned country or city?

Bear in mind that nobody can predict what the experience will be like for you. Every case is different and nobody can totally prepare you for what lies ahead. We all have different tastes. It's like giving advice on restaurants. One person might describe as divine cuisine what somebody else classifies as miserable slop.

• Define how much hardship you are willing to put up with!

Going to the local stream to beat the laundry on a rock was totally beyond discussion as far as I was concerned. A reptile infested place plagued by deplorable hygiene and restroom situations makes many women think at least twice. A visit as a tourist may be acceptable while actually living there is impossible for them to consider. Would it be worth the stress?

After you sifted through the piles of material related to your prospective new home, work through the "Decision-Making" checklist in the back of the book. Based on the information from your studies, assign a number value to the various items. This way you identify your likes, your red flags as well as the areas that you need to get more information on.

Applying what you learned, do you still feel the same way about all of your Must-Haves? What actions or compromises could bring the negative numbers closer to acceptability? Be honest on those matters that are not negotiable.

5) Do a preliminary financial appraisal.

Assuming that the candidate is qualified and interested in the overseas job, how does a family determine whether they can AFFORD to be expats? Many people are willing to make some short-term financial sacrifices in order to sign up for the 'experience of a lifetime.' At what point will the sacrifice become unreasonable and unwise?

• There are some red flags that could tell a candidate that, from a financial point of view, expatriate relocation might not be an option. The following list is certainly not exhaustive, but it could offer some food for thought. Problem areas often encountered are:

> Multiple mortgages,
> sizeable debts,
> legal problems such as bankruptcy,
> other business involvement
>> i.e. partnerships, family business,
>> ownership of rental property ...

• What is the employer's compensation package for expats?

Many employers provide extra allowances to equalize the costs of housing, goods and services, taxes and insurance. They may offer special foreign assignment bonuses. Get a copy of your employer's policy and study it. You must understand the details of the compensation package if you want to get a picture of what your financial situation will be once you relocate.

• How dependent is the family on the spouse's income?

If the family depends on the spouse's salary for sheer survival and if the working partner's pay increase and other compensations do not make up for the difference in income, then you have a problem.

So take an honest look at where the spouse's income is spent. Is the paycheck spent on basics or is it mostly spent on extras: the extra car, the boat, travel, the extra mortgage(s), eating out, hiring a maid, sending the laundry out, financing hobbies, magazine subscriptions?

• Can you cut back on extras and what other spending adjustments can be made?

The time may have come to sort out the family's priorities. Do you want to keep on with the present lifestyle or is it worth your while to do a few creative financial adjustments in order to spend some time overseas?

Excise the fat! In order to cut family expenses, the first recommendation from most financial advisors is to go on a strict credit card diet. Throw out all those catalogues that keep tempting you. If you are a book or CD addict, try to enjoy for a while what you have already rather than succumbing to the continuous spell of new releases.

Go to the beginning of the Checklist section in the back of the book. You find Tables 1 and 2 which illustrate simplified financial examples of two rather typical, fictitious families faced with the decision whether they should go on expat assignment. We have a workable financial situation for the Smith family and a very marginal financial situation for the Robinson family. Both families have 2 elementary school aged children, a house mortgage and 2 cars.

Both families have almost equal combined income. In the Robinson family, however, the spouse contributes a larger portion to the family accounts than in the Smith family. The Robinsons are at a disadvantage once the spouse's income disappears. Their proportional loss will be greater than the Smith's. Besides the Robinsons also carry a significant credit card debt. They will have no financial cushion for emergency and unforeseen expenses. Unless the employer's expat package is truly exceptional, I think that it would be unwise for the Robinsons to accept an expat assignment at this time. Note that for these examples it is assumed that the respective employers would pay the families' additional taxes and housing expenses in case of relocation.

So where do you stand financially? Be courageous! Fill out Table 3 and see for yourself.

- What expenses may increase with expatriate duty?

How much money you spend besides your daily living expenses depends mainly on you. Travel, leisure, photos, souvenirs and telephone bills seem to top the list. Especially in the beginning people are eager to experience new tastes and thus tend to eat out more frequently than they used to.

Some expats ended up sending money home in order to hire help for aging parents. Had they lived at home they could have provided a good portion of these services personally at no extra cost.

Also, repairs to the homestead that one could have done oneself are now hired out and cost more.

- What expenses may decrease with expatriate duty?

While we were on expatriate mission, our transportation costs were sharply reduced. We sold our cars in the U.S., and the company provided us with a lease car. We were billed a flat monthly fee which covered fuel, insurance and maintenance. Had I insisted on having an additional car for my own use, we would have had to pay for that. Luckily I was in a position where I could use public transportation, and better yet, get my wellness points by walking.

- Should you sell your home in order to get some extra cash?

On this topic two basic questions must be asked.

How much do you love your present home?

What do you need the extra cash for?

If you sell your house because you have plans to move somewhere else anyway, you probably have a good opportunity at this point to make a clean break. Generally speaking though, before you sell your home check on the tax implications and review your employer's compensation policy. Different employers handle the homestead question differently.

If you sell your home purely to get extra money so that you can afford to go on an expatriate adventure, you have a big problem.

If you sell your home, keep in mind that you will probably pay more for a comparable home upon your return. Unless you can invest or save the money from the transaction, there could be trouble. The money from the house sale should work for you while you are gone.

If you sell your home, you no longer carry a mortgage, and you also do not receive any rent revenues that could be passed on to the company. In this case many employers make you pay for your living arrangements overseas. Depending on your location, this could amount to a sizeable expense. Houses and apartments with views are at a premium especially in big cities.

If you keep your home, the company should keep you whole. If you pay the mortgage and rent it out during your absence to some friends or to a responsible renter, the company should pay for the difference in the non-homestead insurance and tax rates. In exchange for keeping the rent money from your place, the employer should provide you with an appropriate allowance for your accommodation overseas. Most expats that I talked to operated on this premise.

• Some families save or invest one spouse's income. You must decide whether your portfolios can coast for a while.

If you have a lot of market sensitive investments, it is usually a good idea to get a financial advisor to watch over them while you are overseas. Ask for monthly statements. Get the name and telephone number of your personal advisor. Companies usually do not provide this service, but those of us who signed up privately with a family financial specialist felt that it was worth the money. They provided us not only with the correct statements at tax times but also with some much needed peace of mind.

   • Are there ways of watching the market from overseas on your own?

People with good financial sense do very well for themselves by reading financial publications and by surfing the net. The question is how much do you understand about the market in the first place and how gifted are you in deciphering the financial print? We had so many things to concentrate on that playing the market on our own was not an option.

   6) Is your assignment compatible with your health?
Are there clinics, hospitals or even doctors in the area where you might live? How far away are they? How reliable is the local blood supply?

It is amazing how many people never think about their health before they sign up for expat duty. They worry more about their well-being on a two-week trip to Mexico than they do when faced with spending years in some far-away corner of the world. Yet, health problems on foreign turf can become overwhelming in a hurry.

Since you live in your body 24 hours a day, you alone really know what shape it is in. Expatriate missions have a tendency to complicate the health picture for many candidates. People who need continuous medical care, routine tests and esoteric medications should have a good talk with their physician before they even think about an overseas assignment. Since most countries require a complete physical before they grant temporary entry privileges, a seriously compromised applicant might be rejected during this process. Many places are quite strict and do not tolerate entrants with longstanding medical problems. Lying about your health on visa applications could be a costly venture and render you an enormous disservice.

As your homework provides you with data on your new country, think very carefully about the health situation of the various family members. How well a patient with a chronic condition will fare all depends on the location of the assignment.

Jess, who was stationed in Singapore, spent some miserable days inside because her ASTHMA spun out of control as soon as she stuck her head out the door. The heat, the high humidity and the polluting haze from brush fires in Malaysia kept her prisoner in her apartment. On her first trip home, her medicines were adjusted in a most serious way, and she got clear instructions from the respiratory specialist on how to handle the situation in the future. Eventually she had to be recalled from her post.

ALLERGY sufferers might also consider the tropics with caution due to year-round high pollen and fungal counts. Get some appropriate, non-sedating medication before you leave. Anybody who is highly allergic to insect bites is well-advised to carry an emergency kit with the proper inhalers, injections and other medicines and supplies in case of an emergency.

We were not only tortured by mosquitoes but also by sandflies. The locals told me that sandflies actually pee on the skin and produce a chemical burn. Whatever it was, during our first year the "bites "itched for three weeks. After a while we became somewhat immune to the pests, but I always carried my beloved Hydrocortisone cream in my purse. A skin-numbing gel also provided some relief.

If you are considered for high-altitude living, get some health facts on the subject, especially if you have BREATHING or HEART problems. Depending on the severity of your condition, the Andes and the Himalayas are not the places of choice for such candidates.

Gene who had a slight touch of emphysema had to be reassigned to a lower lying facility in Saudi Arabia. Living in the more mountainous area affected his health adversely and threatened to cancel his assignment.

People who are prone to DEPRESSION do not do well in areas where it will be dark or rainy for months at a time. Iceland, the Scandinavian countries and some locations in northern Europe could well make a miserable condition a lot worse.

Women with HORMONAL problems ranging from killer menstrual cramps to hot flashes are advised to have some fine-tuning done before they hop on the plane. Competent gynecologists are hard to come by even in some of the more developed countries.

In isolated places or Third World countries DIABETICS might find it hard to locate suitable dietary products and equipment such as syringes, insulin, needles and blood testing strips. Even in more affluent areas grocery stores often do not carry large selections of sugarfree products. Special stores for diabetics might have to be located. Check with the local Diabetes Association for details.

How much STRESS will your partner's new position generate? How will his/her high blood pressure, diabetes or nervous condition fare? Will that old ulcer act up again? What about yourself and the kids? How do you all hold up under pressure? Remember that the mere fact of living abroad in an unfamiliar environment adds some extra stress to the equation, especially in the beginning.

Health problems and concerns should weigh very heavily when an employee is faced with a possible expat assignment. We have a tendency to take a lot of conveniences for granted when it comes to health maintenance. Being aware that there might be some problems in this regard is half the battle. Be pro-active and minimize surprises. Talk to your doctor first and find out if your assignment would be compatible with your health.

7) *Will the kids go too?*
Unhappy kids make for an unhappy expat experience!

If two adults are confronted with an overseas assignment, that's one thing. If children are involved in the move, the whole experience changes focus altogether, especially for the spouse. Travel opportunities, such as accompanying the partner on a business trip while on location, will be somewhat curtailed. Personal freedom for lunches or hobbies is also limited by the presence of children. Of course, the same thing would be true at home. But, since you are already overseas, you might feel the urge to profit of the opportunity to see as much as possible of the new land and to dive with gusto into all sorts of activities. Especially the limitations on travel tend to breed some resentment in spouses.

In the expat situation, smaller children are probably easiest to deal with. They go where the parents go. They'll make friends because they are too young to have been spoiled by prejudices and preconceived anxieties. They will miss their neighborhood buddies and their grandparents, but they will get over it. During our expat years it always amazed me how adaptable and cooperative small children actually were.

As kids get older, more hurdles have to be overcome. If you trained them thoroughly in knowing 'their rights' and in asserting their individuality, you might have come to the point of regretting a job well done. Of course it all depends on the child or young adult as to what your experience will be. It is almost impossible to predict the reactions of the younger members of the family.

In general, the challenge starts once children reach the teenage years. They become self-assertive and often resist giving up their friends and lifestyle in order to relocate into some foreign country. The first question they probably ask is WHY do we have to move? The fact that their dad's job depends on it, that it presents a tremendous business opportunity, that it is a smart career move, that it is the chance of a lifetime or that it is a learning experience for all of you does not hold much water for them. Some almost-young-adults have been known to refuse to move. Period. Of course, this throws the family into turmoil. As I have already pointed out earlier, some people simply reject the assignment offer due to 'kid trouble.' Other candidates might make arrangements with relatives or friends so that the renegades have a place to stay. Forcing an unwilling teenager into following you overseas can be an exercise in futility. I saw it tried, and I saw it fail.

The time when teenagers approach the last two years of high school is often considered as a particularly bad time for expat relocation. The turmoil of an overseas move threatens to interfere with decisions on graduation, college choices and career preferences. Then again, some people might say: "Great opportunity to explore the overseas college scene." Whether one has the luxury to take that position depends a lot on the location of the assignment.

No matter what their ages might be, be honest with your kids right from the start. Explain as best you can the reason for the move, what to expect, where and how long you will live overseas. Show them the atlas. Maybe you can find a video at your library that might help illustrate your case. When in doubt, it is best to err on the side of realism. This does not mean that you have to paint a negative or pessimistic picture for them. Simply be open about the fact that you do not know all of the answers either. Tell them that there are a lot of things that you will find out together, as a TEAM, as a family.

Listen to their concerns and include them in some of the family discussions. Don't be depressed if you hear a lot about their anxieties. You will be in for hours of talking and rationalizing. The same subjects are beaten to death, over and over. But these sessions are therapeutic, both for the kids and for the parents. Children do make very valid points and often surprise us with their degree of insight and maturity.

All family members should have an opportunity to vent their feelings and frustrations, including the children. They are part of the adventure as much as the adults are. They also lose their friends and support, their schools and the familiar surroundings of their homes and neighborhoods. They are just as scared of the tremendous change in their lives as anybody else is. Yet, most kids are real troopers and often perform a lot better overseas than those who talked them into the adventure in the first place.

Children do not like to be misled. Be careful with promises unless you know for a fact that you can deliver the goods. A woman had promised her child a pet koala if they moved to Australia. It is illegal to keep koalas as pets. When highly inflated expectations lose their steam, kids will not hesitate to call you a liar. Sitting somewhere on the Hungarian steppes defending your credibility as a parent is not a pleasant experience.

It is also true that kids can create their own fantasies without the parents realizing it.

Anne had talked at length to her teenage daughter Kathy about their relocation to Queensland, Australia. She was quite relieved, but also amazed, to find Kathy so eager to pack and to get on that plane. The reason for all the excitement was that the young lady had seen an area on the map called "Surfers' Paradise." She thought that this was 'quite close' to where they were supposed to go. Sun, surf, bronzed bodies California-style, who knows what she thought? When it turned out that her destination was indeed a small town, hours away from paradise, Kathy totally lost it and hated everything! Her disappointment was so immense that she never recuperated and ended up back home staying with relatives after barely a year overseas. The child had fallen prey to unrealistic expectations!

As you brief your youngsters on the adventure, don't forget to ask them what the experience means to them. Try to diagnose misunderstandings early on. It will save you all a lot of grief.

Different cultures, different rules!

Laws, discipline and accountability often become targets of major disagreements. You might remember the incident when an American youngster spray-painted some cars in Singapore. He got caned! There are still cultures where people of all ages are held responsible for their actions. You break the law, you pay the price, whatever that price is!

No company should send expats on assignment without giving them a thorough briefing on the legal situation at the proposed site. If the laws and customs as well as the punishment for certain types of behavior do not meet with your approval, then do not take the job. Creating international political incidents is not in your own interest nor is it in the interest of your company or of your country.

Talk to your children about the laws in your future home. Laws on drug trafficking and drug use are becoming increasingly tough throughout the world. The jail terms and fines back home pale in comparison to the death penalty imposed by some countries such as Malaysia and Singapore. Children who cannot and will not follow rules, who cannot and will not accept authority or who have behavioral problems that get them consistently in trouble with the law are not good expatriate material.

Test Your Motives and Communicate

By now some the motives that sway people to accept expatriate duty should start to rise to the top.

Test yourself against the most frequently cited reasons for choosing to relocate:

1) Are you ready for a change in your own life?
Might you actually look forward to test some new skills and to face new responsibilities ? If a challenge gets you energized, if you consider an expat assignment because you really want to do it, because it will be a great experience for the whole family, then you have an ideal scenario.

2) Is the timing of the offer good?
We talked about that already. Timing, however, often turns out to be a major factor for people who would like to go on overseas mission and who see the present opportunity as THE chance to do so. Maybe the spouse is not working at this point. Maybe the kids are at a good age. Anyway, it's now or never!

3) Is the assignment a positive career move for your partner and thus of benefit to the family?
In my opinion the completion of a successful overseas tour of duty should never hurt anybody's professional future. On the contrary, exposure to other cultures and ways of doing business might just open some new doors or stimulate some new interests. Broadening one's knowledge and proving that one has an open, flexible mind should never be drawbacks.

There seems to be a bit of a dark side to this motive though. Many people expect that expat duty will give them all sorts of future advantages. They expect a major payoff in the form of financial rewards and promotions. They hope for the corner office in the ivory tower. They feel that their 'sacrifice' should give them an edge over other people at their own level.

On April 14, 1997 *Fortune* magazine published an article by Linda Grant which dealt with some of these often over-inflated expectations. Apparently, around 75% of expatriate managers think of an expatriate tour as a potential major career booster. However, only about 10% are actually promoted when they return to home base. Be prepared that your partner's future might not be with the present employer.

Hoped-for career jumps—which might prove to be elusive dreams—often encourage the spouse to agree to relocation. How can you possibly pass such an opportunity up? The truth is that companies usually do not and cannot guarantee the future. I don't know one single expat who has a clue of what lies ahead for him or her upon going home.

4) Are you afraid to refuse the offer?
Are you afraid that your partner's career will be adversely affected if you declined to relocate? In essence you, the spouse, would become guilty of eliminating future career opportunities for your partner. This is a common fear among expat spouses. One lady said that she did not want to be responsible for messing up her family's future.

It used to be that employees were almost forced to accept job offers if they did not want to upset the boss and if they had plans to stay on the company's movers and shakers list. The days of being sidetracked for refusing an assignment are essentially over. Talk about your doubts and check on the facts ! Human resource departments do not have strategic plans on how to make employees miserable.

5) Do you feel that there is no other option but to accept to relocate?
It is true that a candidate is not given much of a choice by the company if the only position available is an overseas posi-

tion. This happened to Bob. The factory where he worked was scheduled to close. Since he was a valued specialist in his field he was offered a job at a new out-of-country site. With some trepidation, Bob and his wife decided to give expat life a chance. The alternative would have been to secure a letter of recommendation from his boss and to look for opportunities elsewhere. Unlike Bob, Jeff did not accept an overseas posting. He signed on with a different company and is doing very well indeed. There are always options!

Spouses, on the contrary, often feel that they are not given any options by their partners. Sometimes partners want an assignment so badly that they pressure the spouses into accepting an overseas tour regardless of their feelings. This leads to a lot of resentment in the long-run. Don't be a martyr. If you are bullied in not so subtle ways, it is time to have a serious reorientation session with your partner. Never say yes under duress.

Decisions to relocate should not be influenced by feelings of guilt, fear, anxiety and pressure or there will be big trouble ahead. Paranoid and anxious people make paranoid, anxious, unhappy and unreliable expats!

6) Does money play a major role in your decision?
High hopes for terrific financial rewards and tax breaks of all kinds are often cited by candidates when asked why they considered overseas duty. How much money the company pays, how many extras are thrown in varies from case to case. A good negotiator might come up with an exceptional deal. Lynn said it best when she stated that if they were only in it for the money, the family would have done better staying home.

Even though some overseas packages can be pretty tempting, money by itself does not guarantee satisfaction. Don't compromise your minimum requirements for some hoped-for cash. If there is strictly no other thrill in the deal besides the thought of dollar signs, will the prospect of an over-stuffed sock under the mattress carry you through months, years?

Might you be getting combat pay? In the military, difficult and unpleasant assignments are often rewarded with extra cash. If the financial incentive looks too good, look at it again. Will you be sent to an area of political instability or of ethnic strife? Will the assignment be plagued by industrial action and confrontations with unions? If so, no matter how good the pay, they do not pay you enough!

Make sure that there is not a huge gap between what you expect out of the deal and what the assignment actually offers. Remember to check the terms of the employer's compensation package! We discussed all of this already in the chapter on the "Decision Making Process." As far as TAX breaks are concerned it is imperative to separate truth from fiction. Read on. The section on "Practical questions to ask the employer" and the checklist at end of book explore some possible topics to be discussed with the tax specialists.

7) *Do travel opportunities that come with an out-of-country tour tempt you?*

Naturally this is the big carrot dangling in front of every-body's nose. Of course you will travel. Upon your return home you will have a thousand tales to tell, miles of video and stacks of pictures to prove you right. But keep in mind that you are on a working assignment.

The project that my husband was sent on did not allow for much formal vacation. I accompanied him on as many business trips as possible, and we used our weekends wisely. When we returned on home leave we would break up the long flight with some carefully planned stopovers. Even though we did not linger anywhere for too long, we felt that we saw the area. We explored some parts of Asia and the tropical paradises of the South Pacific a few days at a time. We had some lovely experiences and some unforgettable moments on such forays. Sometimes when I got restless, I had to remind myself that we were not on a permanent vacation!

So it might be worthwhile to manage your expectations on the subject of travel. Some spouses had not done so and put tremendous pressure on their partners when the trips were shorter and not as frequent as they had imagined them to be. The partners then felt guilty because of their inability to deliver what the spouse had hoped for.

Spouses also should remember that they will be somewhat tied down by children who have to attend school. If one does not anticipate that this will happen, it can lead to unhappiness and to head-on collisions with school principals.

8) Might you be running away from a situation?
Sometimes an overseas tour can be considered as an opportunity to get away from a messy work situation or from tedious family obligations. Remember that no matter where you go, you take your problems along. Expatriate life tends to worsen unresolved issues. Problems become more unmanageable, not better. In the end, a preoccupied mind and a guilty conscience interfere with job performance and will keep the expats from enjoying their adventure.

As you work through the decision making process, as you test your motives, do not forget to *communicate*! Communicate with your partner, with company representatives, with relocation consultants. Ask questions. If you have concerns, voice them immediately for they will not go away. They will only grow stronger. No money and no hopes for career advantages will take away your worries. Have honest discussions with your partner about all those things that are red flags to you: your doubts, your fears, the pets, the care of aging parents, the health status of certain family members, a child's learning disability. All those issues that keep you tossing and turning at night need to be addressed before you hop on the plane.

HUMOR BREAK

As I just mentioned, when we were on assignment I accompanied my husband as often as possible on some of his business trips. Of course, I feel very lucky that I was able to do so, and the company always made sure that we were well taken care of. Make no mistake, I am quite grateful for the deluxe accommodation that we usually enjoyed. But after a few weeks in even the best of hotels, I felt nickeled and dimed, helpless and extremely frustrated.

THE FIVE STAR HOTEL.

"Good day! Step right in! Treating you well,
is our specialty here at this Five Star Hotel.
Excuse me Sir, but you can't have a view.
Everybody wants one, so what else is new?
Those corporate rates don't buy much at all.
So if you don't mind, you face a brick wall."

The room is too hot. There is not much air.
But look we all got a fake antique chair!
The bed is too soft, the headrest's a brick.
But the design on the duvet is oh so très chic!
I've run out of undies and feel out of sorts.
For three bucks a piece the valet launders shorts.

Is it the Scot in me or maybe the Dutch,
but such highway robbery is simply too much.
By now I don't care how much I stink.

I do my own wash right here in the sink.
I splash on a dash of Chanel's Nineteen
which makes even the ripest camper smell clean.

I want a club soda, but for some ice
I have to call room service, isn't that nice?
A tip of two dollars, come on lady please,
a five is minimum, don't be such a tease!
They say when you're hungry, let the chef help.
He makes yummy pancakes of polenta and kelp.

"How about a plain sandwich?" I stutter and ask,
but the waiter immediately takes me to task.
"Such a request, Madame, is not quite à propos,
please try the buttercrust bloody rare tournedos."
After two weeks of torture, I'm flat on my back.
My gallbladder strikes. My body's off track.

It 's six in the evening—but if I make my own bed
the maid who is late will get very upset!
The only thing premium around here is my bill.
I sign on the line and wish I could kill!
Call me a taxi, I've been treated too well
and get me out of this Five Star Hotel.

The Plot Thickens: You Are Interested

By now you have spent a lot of time studying up on your
prospective country. You have discussed the advantages and
the pitfalls of the assignment ad nauseam with family and
friends. You have talked to the children and of course to your
partner. You thought about your motives. You feel that they
are pure and strong enough to keep you fired-up for years.
After some initial stumbling blocks have been cleared out of
the way, the decision has become a lot easier. Yes, you are interested in becoming an expatriate!

In the end, you go on expatriate tour not so much because of money or promotions but

- because you simply want to,
- because you are eager to learn about other cultures, places and about yourself,
- because it is a new, exciting and challenging experience,
- because it is an opportunity of a lifetime for yourself and for the kids,
- because it is a chance for personal growth and satisfaction,
- because you want to expand your horizon and get the braces off your brain,
- because it is right for you.

After you have come to the conclusion that you will support your partner if he/she is considered as a candidate, the human resource department will become very interested in you. They have all sorts of questions to ask you but there are also some that you should ask them.

Practical Questions to Ask the Employer

First, never assume that employers will 'take care' of you ! They provide certain services for their expats, but a lot is left for the individuals to deal with. You know yourself and your family. You know your priorities and needs. Stay in charge of your own life. Ask questions and do not assume.

By the way, did you get a copy of your employer's expat compensation package yet? If not get one now. There is a lot of studying to be done!

Here are some concerns that many of us wished we had addressed ahead of time. Then again, when we all went through our interviews we did not realize that these issues would become problems.

1) *What is your exact immigration status in your host country?*
- Resident? Non-resident? Temporary entrant? Other?
- What are your rights? Limitations?
- Will your classification allow you, the spouse, to work? If so, what special permits and papers have to be secured?
- Do you have to leave the host country for a certain period of time every year?

Misinformation and misunderstandings regarding immigration matters abound among expats. When I had to fill out the immigration forms on the plane, it became clear that I did not know what my status was. The topic had never come up for discussion.

2) *Who will prepare your taxes?*
Providing a tax service for expatriate employees is both basic and vital. Preparing international tax returns can be a nightmare for the lay person. An already tedious task is further complicated by foreign language and alphabet issues as well as by foreign tax and legal requirements. So leave it to the professionals. Get the name of your personal consultant and meet with him or her personally. This is very important because there are a lot of questions to be answered. Schedule plenty of time for the appointment and take a big notebook.

Following are a few recurring points of confusion that should stimulate interesting discussions between yourself and your tax representative.

Basically, we have to look at two different scenarios:
- The expat retains U.S. residency and works for a U.S. company for a limited time overseas.
- A U.S. citizen gives up residency in the U.S. and works for an overseas company.

This second case is often cited as being a real money

maker. But there are a lot of strings attached to tax breaks and tax shelters. Shifting residency to countries with lower tax rates than the U.S. or even without any income tax requirements at all tend to appeal to the dollar-wise. Before leaving check on the tax regulations both at home and abroad and stay on the good side of the law.

Ponder the following issues as they apply to your case with your tax advisor.

- Do you have to pay U.S. taxes even though you live and work overseas? What about state and local taxes?
- Does your company have a tax equalization policy?

Such a policy offers excess tax protection to the employee. It equalizes the taxes paid by expatriates. A hypothetical tax is computed as if the expat were residing in the U.S. paying only domestic taxes. The employer pays all excess taxes resulting from the foreign assignment.

- Do you have to pay taxes in your host country?
- Do you need a tax filing number in your host country? Where do you apply to get one?
- Is it true that your host country might tax the revenues from investments and savings that you have in the U.S.? Will the U.S. tax your revenues from possible foreign investments?
- How can you ease the tax burden both at home and abroad?!
- How does the length of your assignment impact your tax situation? Is there a limit on the number of years that you can remain an expat?
- What if you wanted to stay longer in your host country?
- Do you have to be out of the U.S. for a specified time to qualify for tax advantages?
- What happens if you come back early?

- Will it be an advantage if the spouse works overseas, provided that all permits and laws are complied with?

We would have actually been at a serious financial disadvantage if I had worked for pay. After going through all of the stress of getting a license to practice and a working permit, it would have almost cost me money to be able to work.

A friend of mine who is a professional artist had an opportunity to work for pay while overseas. Her income though would have been taxed both at home and in her host country. After a financial analysis, she would have made barely enough to pay for the materials she needed in order to complete the projects. She rejected the deal.

Of course every case is different. But before you get all excited about your chance to pad the family wallet, make sure that your efforts do not actually empty it.

- Since tax years vary, by what time must you have your filing documents ready?
- If there are filing problems or delays that are not your fault, who assumes responsibility and pays the fines?
- Is there any tax advantage to owning property overseas?

Regardless of what the tax laws say, trying to speculate on overseas property has caused a lot of stress to some expats. First, an expat is usually not long enough in a particular area in order to get a good handle on the market. I have seen money being lost by folks who invested in promising development projects that ultimately went bust. Who actually owns the property that you plan to buy? Getting embroiled in battles with local government agencies, environmentalists, villagers or even warlords is an other reason why foreign land deals can make blood pressures rise. The bottom line is: if you buy, be sure that you know the market and that you get the tax and legal details sorted out ahead of time.

• Do you have to pay back taxes after your return? Federal? State? Local?

Laws vary from state to state. Have the tax details—both domestic and foreign—that apply to your contract thoroughly explained by a specialist. An acquaintance from an eastern state did not move back to her home state once her assignment was over. She would have gotten 'killed' with back taxes. Therefore she relocated across the state line.

3) Will the company pay for a financial adviser?
Usually companies do not provide this service for the average employees. It is up to the individuals to decide whether their financial situation warrants the expense.

4) If you keep your home:
• Will the company pay the non-homestead differences in property tax and insurance rates?
• Who will get the rent money?

If the company pays for your accommodation overseas, they will probably retain the rent on your house back home.
• When you move back, will you get a painting and cleaning allowance?
• Who will manage your property? Will the company provide this service?

Meet personally with your property manager. Before you leave take care of the details regarding lease agreements. Trying to arrange these items via telephone or fax leaves a lot of room for error and frustration. Also, make an effort to find your own renters. It alleviates a lot of anxiety if you know the people personally who occupy your home in your absence.
• How often will your property be inspected?
• Will you be given a report after such inspections?
• Discuss the current service contracts that you have for your house.

These might include lawn and garden maintenance, snow

shoveling, appliance service and repair, window washing and so on. Do you want these services continued? Notify the service providers of your move. If applicable, give them the name of the property manager who will be their new contact person in the future.

5) *If you sell your home:*

• How much help will your company provide in case that the sale is not completed by the time you leave? Will the company buy your house at fair market price in case of delayed sales? Remember to discuss the Capital Gains taxes with your tax advisor before you leave!

• If the company encourages you or even tells you to sell your home, how will they make you 'whole' at the end of your contract? Will you get an allowance to bridge the gap between property prices? You obviously will pay more for a comparable home upon your return.

6) *What is the cost of living in your host country?*

• Is your allocated expense budget rational considering the cost of living in your assigned country?

• Is your pay adjusted for cost of living?

People tend to be shocked by how much life costs in places like Japan or Norway. But in rural or isolated areas where housing is scarce and supplies have to be flown in, basic living can cost a mint.

• Get the exact figures of what your allowance is for accommodation, transportation and furniture rentals.

Allowances vary depending on such things as the location of the assignment and the level of your partner's position. Don't find out too late that you overstepped your limits. A lady told me that they selected their furniture unaware of their spending limits. When they found out that they had gone overboard, the order had been placed and they made up the difference out of their own pocket.

7) What are the pay arrangements for your partner?

• Will you have to transfer money (very aggravating) between your account at home and your account overseas or will the pay be split: so much to the bank account at home, so much to the local account?

• What currency will your partner be paid in? This is a very important issue especially if the currency in your host country is unstable. Talk to the accountants about this.

8) Will the company compensate you in any way for the loss of the spouse's income?

Such compensation is not standard practice for most employers. Yet, in order to make expatriate assignments more palatable to dual career couples, some companies have started to offer limited packages such as paying out a few months of the spouse's base pay as a lump sum. Other employers might provide more supportive care such as help with résumés or job hunting. Usually though compensation for lost income is not offered.

9) Who will pay the school tuition if you choose to send your child to a private school because the local public schools are inadequate?

10) Will your household goods at home be stored?

• Will the company pay for this service?

• Is there a limit on the amount that you are allowed to store?

• Are there items that storage companies might refuse to store?

Pianos, cars, explosives, guns, valuable art pieces and fragile, costly electronic equipment might figure among the exclusions.

• How accessible are your goods?

Some expats have found that it took an act of God to gain access to their storage facility. Besides having to give plenty of advance notice, penalties had to be paid for removing items before the end of the contract?

   • Are your goods insured and is the insurance sufficient?

   11) Clarify the health insurance issue.
It is absolutely crucial to get some crystal clear answers to health insurance matters!!

   • Where do you go when you get ill?

Will you deal with a special expat clinic or do you use the emergency room at a local hospital? Get specific guidelines on how to access medical care in your host country.

Are there any health care facilities such as clinics, hospitals and doctors in your area? Can you trust the hygiene at the facilities? If you need an injection, can you trust that the needles are clean? What is the level of expertise of the local physicians? How far away are the nearest specialists?

   • Who pays when you get ill?

Will your company provide for on-site private coverage for you and your family? If so, what exactly is covered ? Major medical? Medications? Dental? Optical? Ambulance services? Psychological care? Pregnancy? Intensive care? What is the exact name of the insurance company? Where are they located? What is the emergency number in your area? Who is your contact person? Review these details with a Human Resource representative before leaving.

Even if you are insured overseas, don't let your current policy at home lapse. There is the old rule that states: "Once you got health insurance, hang on to the policy."

Some expats that I met had been told by their companies that they would qualify for the public health coverage in Australia. While it is true that Australia, at least at that time, had a reciprocal agreement with some countries for short-term, emergency care for their citizens (up to 6 months), it was wrong to assume that anybody who paid taxes was covered.

In order to qualify for coverage on the public system one had to be resident of the country. Expats generally do not have resident status.

If you are covered by the company through a policy at home, who will be your health liaison person at the home office?

Get a name and telephone number because you will need this person's help in case of problems with the filing procedures. Long distance claims that lack the proper code numbers and feature receipts involving foreign language, alphabet and currency are not what the average claims clerk is used to. Ideally, the home-based insurance company or HMO has been contacted ahead of time and is familiar with your special expat needs and status. Get the name and number of someone in the claims department that you will be dealing with. Obtaining an after-hours number for either the home office or the insurance provider could also be most helpful since illnesses and emergencies do not always happen conveniently during office hours.

Just about all of the expats that I know needed medical care while overseas. Medical bills spiral out of control relatively fast, and the providers expect to be paid in a timely fashion. The question that always arose was : where do I get the bundle of money from in order to cover these expenses? Will the company advance you the cash to pay on the spot for medical care? Do you put the bills on your expense account and settle the matter with the accountants later? We all know that even under the best of circumstances it takes months to get any action out of health insurance companies. Dealing with such frustrations at home is bad enough. Dealing with them from abroad is agony.

When one of our expats went to the hospital, he had to hand the cashier his credit card before he was admitted for emergency surgery. That's scary. So, ask questions and take detailed notes!!

• Did your employer sign you up with up with an international emergency plan such as the SOS International Assistance services? If you need to be flown back to civilization or if you need help in an emergency situation, this could be a good start. But it is not health insurance for daily living. Also, make sure that your emergency plan has an office and a 24-hour number in your general area. The usefulness of such emergency services is sometimes debated, but I know of families who got some much needed help from them. Carrying a card with some contact numbers 'just in case' makes expats breathe a bit easier.

Besides unpredictable mail services, the health insurance issue probably caused the most stress and frustration in our group of exiles. Don't think that anybody knows anywhere else in the world what to do with your managed care insurance card. We simply paid for some everyday care out-of-pocket, because it was not worth the time or the aggravation to file long distance with some unresponsive group on a different continent.

• Does the company provide access to counseling services should the need arise?

Remember that the unforeseen can throw an otherwise stable expat right off the surfboard. In case of a family crisis even a long distance telephone call with a professional can alleviate all kinds of anxieties. When the chips are down, we want to phone home. Employers should have a professional group or an individual already picked. It is not a good time to thumb through the yellow pages in search of help once calls start coming in from panicky expats. Ask for names!

Expatriates are often reluctant to confide in local psychologists or counselors. They may question the expertise of such professionals. They may feel that there is little understanding for their unique situation. In small towns doubts about confidentiality also arise.

12) *If you relocate into a country where you are allowed to drive, do you need to get a local driver's license?*

Even if you do not, get a copy of the traffic rules and study it thoroughly. Don't try to improvise.

13) *Clarify the car insurance issue!*

This is a very important issue that often is not addressed at all before the expat leaves. It is very distressing to find out after the fact that the insurance is insufficient and out of compliance with local laws. Don't take sketchy details for an answer.

• What insurance does the company provide? Is there a group policy? A personal liability policy? Are you left on your own?

• Is your car rented or leased? Will you buy your own?

Chances are that the car will be leased for your tour of duty. Check that you have both liability and collision insurance and that your license is legal. Don't get tripped by insurance loopholes. Read the fine print so that you understand what your personal responsibilities are.

If the car is simply rented, either overseas or while on home leave, buy the insurance unless you have irrefutable proof that you are indeed covered by a company group policy. Get the facts! Obtain the name of the insurance company, the terms of the policy and the policy number before you leave. Don't be satisfied with the statement: "If you rent a car, charge it on your company-issued credit card and you are covered." Oh, so simple! Do you have a phone number on whom or where to call in case of need? What is the extent of the coverage? Is there a time limit for such coverage? Know what that limit is. In our case it was 31 days from the time of rental on Visa, 15 days on MasterCard. Be sure that the information that you receive is both complete and correct!

Many countries take the guesswork right out of the car rental situation by mandating that you buy comprehensive coverage when renting a vehicle regardless of which credit card is used.

Use common sense when renting a vehicle on unfamiliar territory. Limit night driving. Rent the safest car you can get and make sure that there are working seat belts. Safety standards that we take for granted are often not required in other countries.

A word of caution about left-side driving!

While Jeff was an expat in the United Kingdom, he got into a head-on collision. Driving on the left side of the road did not cause him any particular problem. One day though, as he tried to avoid a traffic hazard, he pulled to the right, into the way of oncoming cars. When faced with danger we tend to react in a reflex-like manner, the way it was drilled into us.

In Scotland Sue got on the wrong side of the road as she pulled out of the parking lot in a shopping center.

An Australian lady told me that she lost her favorite nephew in a fatal crash in the U.S. He died on a country road somewhere out west. He obviously never realized that he was driving for miles on the wrong side of the road until he met up with the truck.

Assuming that you have a car with the steering wheel on the correct side for the system that you are in, remember that *the driver always sits towards the middle of the road.* That is true for both the left-side and the right-side driving situations. If the driver rides along the ditch, the car is on the wrong side of the street.

Driving is one of the biggest liabilities faced by expats. Different traffic patterns and rules, different language on signs, driving on the opposite side of the road, all contribute to making the expat very vulnerable. Traffic mishaps and deaths are a greater threat to an expat's (or traveler's) safety and health than all the weird diseases combined.

14) How much preparation relevant to your assignment will your company provide?

Don't let anyone tell you: "Oh, you'll catch on fast. Nobody can really prepare you anyway. It's best to simply jump right in!" Forget it! Even though you can do quite a bit of exploratory work on your own, you still need the help and support of the home office.

• If needed, will you be instructed in the language and alphabet of your host country?

By the time you stumble off the plane, you should be able to read simple signs, the menu in the restaurant and other important pieces of information. Basic, or maybe not so basic, full language courses are expensive and should be made available. Being able to communicate takes some of the isolation and lonesomeness out of the assignment and will make your life a lot easier. It also tears down at least some of the barriers that language throws up between people and thus softens the culture shock. It is true that a friendly smile has its charm, but saying "thank you" and "please" to your hosts in their own language will take you a long way.

• Will the company offer some seminars to familiarize yourself with the culture and the protocols of your host country?

I mentioned before that companies often get carried away worrying about the success of their business venture and forget that business failures often start with a faux pas on the social scene. They might prepare the partner for the new business climate with classes on contracts, finances, and negotiating tricks. But in the heat of the passion they often fail to instruct both the candidate and the family in matters such as social protocol and hierarchy or body language. Yet, a major ingredient for a successful mission abroad is to send an expat team that is capable of functioning comfortably in their new environment. Once again, get the odds on your side and don't go unprepared!

15) *How many home visits does the company pay for per year?*

Many employers offer spouses and children one yearly trip home traveling business class. Some folks make a deal to fly economy if this allows them to go home twice. Since travel arrangements can be a major cause of unhappiness, most expats nowadays are given a yearly travel allowance to spend at their own discretion.

16) *Is emergency travel (going home for a family crisis) included in the travel allowance or is that extra?*

Emergency travel should ideally be extra. Secure your deals before you leave.

17) *Will the company pay for the spouse/family when the partner has to go on extended business trips?*

The answer to this question depends a lot on how long the partner will be gone, how many people in the family would have to travel and how liberal the company is with money. Usually companies will not pay extra for whole families to travel under such circumstances.

18) *Can you take the pets and, if so, will the company pay for the transfer?*

As a rule, it is best to find a new, good home for animals. Some countries do not allow pets at all, some have prolonged quarantine requirements. The latter would have been our case. If we had decided to take our cats along, poor Smithers and Cinna would have been isolated for up to nine months! It was better to place them with an other loving owner. Who would have taken care of them anyway when we went home on vacation or when we traveled?

19) *Will the company pay for all those extras such as electrical appliances that you have to purchase? What about all the other goods such as drapes or bedding?*

Electrical voltage and phase differences make the transfer of equipment somewhat tedious. Many companies give their expats a relocation allowance. That way everybody can decide what items have priority status: lamps, fans, bread-makers or fine silks?

20) *Will the employer help pay for your long distance calls when you phone home?*

I never found any expats who enjoyed such utter luxury. Basically, you chat on your own nickel. Write, E-mail, make arrangements with your family to call you once in a while or sign up with a discount long distance company. Phone allowances are very rare if they exist at all.

Site Visit: The Final Test

Once a candidate is a serious prospect, an inspection visit of the assigned site is usually arranged. Companies, however, take a risk by letting people have a preliminary peek at their future location. No matter what the place looks like, chances are that the candidate and his/her family do not find it perfect enough and thus turn the assignment down. Then the whole search process has to start all over. That is very costly.

A tactic that is best avoided is to act like George. Even though he later admitted that he had no intention to relocate, he 'squeezed' a free trip out of the company by suggesting that he was interested. Such unfair and dishonest make-believe unfortunately happens. This type of sharpness maliciously wastes thousands of company dollars and does not endear the perpetrator to anybody. George lost the respect of his co-workers and started hunting for another job.

Bill and his wife were all excited to relocate on a different continent. They did not do any preliminary research about the place, nor did they think ahead of time of the implications that overseas relocation invariably brings. When they embarked on their site visit it was understood that their move was a done deal. Bill met with the business partners and his assignment was approved by them. Then, on the way home, the couple began to think about the kids who would have to change schools, the pets who had no home, the house that would have to be sold and so on! It was a bad scene. By the time they got off the plane, they had decided that the expat duty was not for them. The business project was threatened by the decision. Bill and his wife went through some major trauma which could have all been avoided had they thought rationally about the offer right from the start.

I have to add that often expats go on assignment without the benefit of a site visit. We did. It is up to the candidates and their families to decide for themselves whether expat life is for them and to commit to the job, site unseen. In their hearts, people know right from the start whether they might consider a transfer to the proposed location. If they are curious and motivated enough, they do their homework ahead of time. They evaluate their family situation and make up their minds about the job itself. Frankly, if a candidate and his/her family have no clue as to what their decision will be and wait around for the trip to give them the answer, we have a bad situation.

On-site visits can go either way, no matter how much preparing you have done. The physical and psychological impact of findings such as smells, poverty, pollution, isolation or climate cannot be adequately described in books. No television program can ward off culture shock. Each individual has his/her own reaction.

Once you have done your investigating, your first stay in the host country will either alleviate or reinforce your fears and reservations. Disastrous first visits happen most frequently to candidates who have not done any background research and thus do not have their expectations tuned. Going anywhere, even to Paris, without any factual information or interest is a setup for disappointment. In any case, it is also a waste of time, effort and money.

People who are unprepared start to compare everything they see or hear to 'how it is at home.' Suddenly, the grocery store is not like home, the scenery is not like home, people do not dress the way they do at home. Anyone who does this routinely should analyze his/ her feelings thoroughly with regard to overseas assignments. A successful expat has to get out of that frame of mind. No place is perfect, not even 'home,' and no place is totally without charm. Many people have spent years in misery trying to get used to living away from home. By the time they took to the idea, their assignment was over.

If you are lucky enough to get a site inspection, prepare and use your time wisely. Beside looking over the country side and meeting the business partners, try to sort out the real estate and school situations.

Stake out the area and talk to some local real estate people or relocation consultants. It will take a huge worry off your mind if you have at least some idea ahead of time of where you might live.

If you are assigned to company owned housing or to a foreigners' compound, some big decisions have been made for you. The disadvantage is that you have little or no choice where you will spend the next few months or years. If you can have any input at all, live where you, the spouse, would like to live.

The spouse spends a lot more time at home than the working partner. This is why the living accommodations play a big part in expat life. Some people like a place with a view. Others do not care what they look at as long as they are close to town, to a shopping mall or a golf course. Gardens can be considered a must for those spouses blessed with green thumbs or for families whose children have come along.

Whatever accommodation you choose, take care not to

become a prisoner in your own dwelling. My friend Sue once described her house as a 'jail.' What a sentence! Mary lived way out in the boonies just because her partner liked the peace and quiet whenever he was home. So guess where Mary was all day long? Isolated in the sticks nursing a case of melancholy.

Our assignment took us to a small harbor town. I forfeited the benefits of a newer home with master bedroom suite and central air for an older house which gave me an excellent view of the ocean. Even though I spent a lot of time by myself, watching the tug boats go to work and the overseas ships sail by kept me connected in some odd way to the world and saved my sanity many times.

The location of your new home often determines how mobile you, the spouse, will be. I endeavored to remain as independent as possible. It was very important to me to have easy access to downtown, the grocery store and a bus line. I could never really depend on having our leased company car. Because of the type of job that my husband had, our car sharing arrangements became obsolete within weeks. But, since we were centrally located, this only meant that I had to do a bit more planning and walking. I had the time, and I needed the exercise! Getting a second car just for me would have been at our expense and in my mind a waste of money and a big headache.

Some countries solve all transportation problems for you. You hire local drivers. Foreigners are not allowed behind the wheel due to tedious traffic situations, language and alphabet problems. Other places do not allow women to drive. Needless to say, some activities that we take for granted, such as moving about independently, can become major challenges elsewhere. Whether you drive yourself, ride the bus, have a driver or walk, choose your location carefully so that you do not isolate yourself unnecessarily.

As parents your next challenge is to check out the schools and to talk to some of the teachers while you are on site visit. The kids either go to special expat schools or they attend the local schools. Problems involving the education system frequently cause major concerns among expats. Lack of quality education is one of the family issues that convinces candidates to turn down out-of-country assignments.

Here are a few issues that have caused mayhem in the past:

- Courses required for re-entry into high school, college or university back home are either not offered or cannot be transferred because the curriculum is substandard or not accredited. This can delay someone's graduation or academic career substantially. Math, science, second language courses, lab work as well as up-to-date computer classes are known problem areas.
- The specific year that your child is supposed to register for is not offered. One family whose teenager was to enter year 12 in an expat international school found out that year 12 was not yet offered at that facility. The youngster finally stayed with the grandparents back home in order to finish his last year of high school.
- Teaching and discipline styles tend to become major stumbling blocks. We train our students to be confident, to have an opinion, to express themselves and to be a team player. Traditional schools where the teacher talks and the pupil sits quietly often do not score high marks with U.S. students in general. Conversely, foreign teachers tend to think of our kids as noncompliant individualists.

I know of an eleven-year-old boy who had to be literally dragged to school by his distraught parents because he hated so much going there. The ritual repeated itself every day until he was sent home to live with relatives while the parents tried to get out of their contract. Needless to say, breaking the signed agreement was an action that did not endear them to the head office and it cost them a considerable chunk of cash. In retrospect, it seems that this child was badly prepared for being thrown into an expat situation in the first place.

- Uniforms tend to be unpopular with U.S. children. Yet in many countries both public and private schools strictly enforce them. Until the child gets used to the idea, it is a real drag to fight the same battle over and over, day after day.

Patty's daughter Lisa caused her parents a lot of added unexpected stress. Every single morning—as she put on her regulation knit knee-high stockings and below-the-knee skirt—she cried and threw a tantrum. The outfit did not do a thing for a young girl's self-esteem. We all agreed on that, but it did not matter. Rules were rules. Patty tried to talk to the principal. He wondered what the problem was? Nobody else had this kind of reaction. Why could the parents not get a bit tougher?

What came to this American teenager as a shock was simply a given reality to the local children. They knew that going to that particular school meant that one had to wear that particular uniform. Education versus frock: what is more important? In the end, Lisa switched to a different school. Maybe she learned less, but the uniform requirements were less strict.

If you have a chance to talk to some school officials, find out what is expected of you as a parent and of the child as a student. Eliminate surprises. It will make life so much easier.

I have known people who got themselves into trouble with the local schools because they let kids skip classes for days for the purpose of travel. This practice is usually frowned upon. We like to say that children learn more on a trip than they do in a classroom anyway, but be really cautious how much you use that excuse. Teachers have a tendency to get peeved if they sense that you make light of their efforts. Also, continuously requiring exceptional status will make the children's lives a lot harder.

Expat parents have been told in no uncertain terms that, if they expected their youngsters to attend classes or to even graduate from the local system, rules had to be obeyed. Letters of recommendation and of attendance have been denied due to excessive absenteeism. Before taking your children out of school, come to an understanding with the teachers and with the policy makers. Be sure that everybody shares your enthusiasm for independent study.

Once you have familiarized yourself with the sights, sounds and customs of your prospective new home, listen to the little voice inside of you. Be honest in your evaluation and say what you truly feel. Do you see yourself living in this place? When all is said and done, the real question still is: do you want to commit to an overseas assignment in this location? Remember that employers look for commitment from the assigned employee as well as from his/her family. Rightfully so.

Should it happen that in theory the tour of duty sounded like a good idea but that in practice you cannot handle it, then speak your mind as soon as possible. Companies are not in the business of making employees and their families unhappy, nor do they relish the thought of dumping their workers into the laps of divorce lawyers. They do, however, appreciate your honesty. Assignments can be changed, compromises can be made but the company representatives have to know about your concerns.

After you have looked at all the data, come to a decision that the whole family can live with. You should be at peace with your choice. If overseas duty is out of the question in your case, so be it! You have made an informed, honest decision. You have done a fine job!

But let's say that your arduous research and a successful site visit have inspired you to partake of the proposed adventure. YOU ACCEPT!

Congratulations! Keep that positive attitude! You have started to ride the wave!

Depending on your assignment, this is the time that you will be invited to attend special classes where you learn about the history, the language and the customs of your future 'home' in great detail and from a practical point of view. There is a lot of work ahead, but you are almost there!

III

Yes We Are Going— How Do We Prepare?

Understand the Different Emotional Waves

Expatriate assignments are often described as emotional roller-coasters. Riding such emotional waves is a skill that has to be tackled by anyone who decides to navigate the surf of expatriate life.

The cycles of up-and-down swings are not only a part of the initial relocation or departure phase of expat life. Just as one ocean wave rolls into the next, expats will encounter the surges again after they arrive in the new land and also as they prepare to return to the homeland.

Before I dive into the various chapters, let me give you a brief explanation of Figure #1. I basically describe the different stages that I identified in my own situation and that other expats certainly endorsed. Not all of these emotions might hit you at exactly the same time and in exactly the same way as they hit me. Simply remember to hug your surfboard whenever you get discouraged. Things will get better. If you find yourself riding a huge high, don't let go of the surfboard. A destabilizing emotional wave might be ahead.

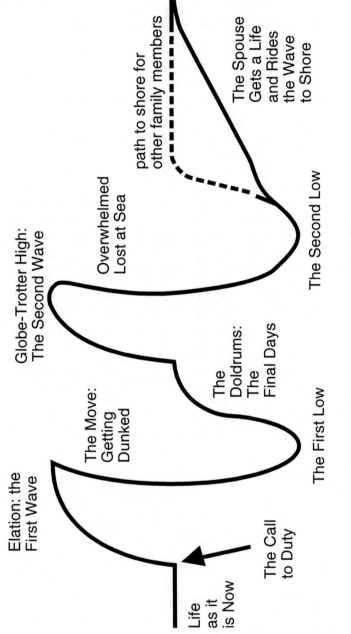

Life as it is Now

The Call to Duty

Elation: the First Wave

The Move: Getting Dunked

The Doldrums: The Final Days

The First Low

Globe-Trotter High: The Second Wave

Overwhelmed Lost at Sea

path to shore for other family members

The Second Low

The Spouse Gets a Life and Rides the Wave to Shore

The Emotional Waves
Figure #1

One day your daily routine is upset by the offer of an ex-patriate tour of duty. At first you might be stunned, but then you gradually take to the idea. You begin to ride the upswing of the 'elation wave.'

Next, you are faced with the big move. This is a wake-up call. Before you know it you are in deep water, getting dunked. You head for the first trough. This too shall pass. You'll emerge a bit shaken, ready to coast into a more sedate period before you actually leave. You have hit the pre-departure 'doldrums,' the final days in the old place.

As you step onto the plane, you catch the next up-wave, 'the globe-trotter high.' Yes, the adventure of a lifetime is now ever so near. You look for your tourist brochures in your backpack. You arrive on location ready to go and do things.

The next treacherous wave is sneaking up on you. As you set up your life in a foreign land, you feel somewhat 'lost at sea' amidst all of your new duties and responsibilities. You might even mourn your past and feel unspoken regret. The second low is coming right up. Just hang on!

You will successfully 'ride the wave to shore' once you decide that you have indeed found a new home, once you let go of the past, once you get a life.

Now you are comfortable in your surroundings. You feel good about your mission, and here it is time to go home. Back to the drawing board! At first you are excited. But it saddens you to leave your host country behind. You are in for an other move! You realize that the huge change that repatriation brings will test your surfing skills once more. Up and down! Get ready for the final emotional wave in the raging surf of expat life.

The Elation Wave

Once they recover from their initial bewilderment, most people react with excitement to the prospect of an overseas assignment. Everybody yearns for a change now and then. Who wants to go stale like old bread? People like to have 'things happen' in their lives. An out-of-country experience tends to appeal not only to the tourist within them but also to their sense of adventure. They can see themselves basking on the sandy beaches in some tropical paradise, star gazing in the Sahara desert, tossing coins into world-famous fountains. They immerse themselves in pamphlets and brochures. This expatriate experience seems to be designed just for them!

Don't be amazed if some friends and acquaintances react with envy to the news that you are going places. They do not think about the potential risks that you take. They just know that you are given a unique opportunity to enrich your life while they stay behind in the old rut. It is human nature that this type of response might make you feel quite privileged. You suddenly realize that you got something that other people might also want but are not offered. Now that's excitement!

Visits to the expat liaison person—a blend of travel/sales agent and talent recruiter—figure on your agenda. Magazines, fliers and all sorts of reading materials designed to get you fired up, inundate your kitchen table. The tourist within you comes alive. All the fuss gives you a well-deserved feeling of importance. You almost have celebrity status. Yes! What a feeling! You just caught the upswing of the elation wave!

HUMOR BREAK
PACKING FOR THE MOVE

We got our orders. It is time to pack.
The work, the confusion, Good Lord I'm a wreck!
I paste little stickers in blue and in red:
This stays, this goes!—Should I take my bed?

The tourist within me, is it alive? Is it dead?
Ouch, that chair bonked me right in the head.

I got all my china, my cutlery too.
"The piano? Dear lady, now that is taboo!"
The foreman assures me that I am in luck.
They toss all that stuff with great care on the truck.
"Underhanded," he says, "that's the secret you see.
Guaranteed little breakage is our house policy."

I breathe a deep sigh of enormous relief.
I got my assurance right there from the chief.
The boxes are packed. The place is a mess.
I almost surrendered due to all of this stress.
My pictures, my books, my treasures, my pride
are in, I dare say, for one heck of a ride.

Getting Dunked— The Big Move

Once the decision is made that you all accept the overseas assignment you can sit back and relax! Wrong!! Now the real work begins. Reality calls. An emerging feeling of apprehension should not get a good spouse down! Don't worry! Your initial excitement only experiences a temporary lull. The elation will bloom again once you see the end of the work that lies ahead.

Nan spoke for all of us when she described her feelings that warned of the oncoming trough: "Boy, did I get a wake-up call from one day to the next! I became totally overwhelmed by all those decisions and details, the packing, the travel arrangements, the paperwork! I began to wonder what I got myself into."

Preparation for expat duty might make you feel as if you were taking a 5-credit crash college course. So much information to assimilate and to process in so short a time!

George felt that the tone of urgency that marked the calls from the company's human resource representative reminded him a lot of those that he received years ago from his military recruiter.

Yes, there is plenty to do before you set foot on the plane. Piles of official documents have to be signed, sealed and sent off to the embassy and to various ministries of your host country.

The stress and the commotion caused by the impending move usually herald an imminent emotional downturn. Since the partners with the work assignment are usually shipped out as soon as possible, it often falls on the spouses to take care of the transfer details. This is a daunting process, to say the least, and demands a serious amount of energy and of concentration. Spouses who shoulder the responsibility for a smooth transition all by themselves might voice some early feelings of doubt. At this point it is not difficult to get a bit depressed. Is that amazing? Having been there myself, I hardly think so!

My dining room table had disappeared under mounds of instruction books, lists and manifests. I started to separate all the papers into files so that I would be able to keep the mess somewhat organized. The telephone rang almost continuously: the property manager, the embassy, the house insurance agent, the storage company, the human resource people..! Heeelp! We ran into snags with our travel documents. This called for extra trips to the office, extra runs for pictures and signatures. Like Nan, I began to wonder why I put myself through so much work and confusion. Simply think of this period of upheaval and of chronic fatigue as a transition time that is part of the package. It will soon be over. Keep right on working, stay on that surfboard and don't get dunked! There are calmer waters ahead.

At what point the emotional rapids come into view

depends very much on the individual. People with a matter-of-fact, positive attitude might zoom through this initial period of change without an ambiguous thought in their minds. They simply look forward to the future and consider all the preparation as a necessary prelude to a very unique experience.

Overseas relocation is a convoluted, complicated process. One does not just throw a few things into boxes, call the movers and presto! Even though my husband and I had made some major inroads into the moving process before he left, my initial confidence gradually shattered under the weight of the intricate details and of the continuous surprises that nobody had prepared me for. Other spouses who shared their experiences agreed: we did not know what to expect! We all handled the task, but our lives would have been a lot easier if we had been able to anticipate some of the challenges.

Here are some tips for your move:

First, keep in mind that everything that you send overseas has to come back at the end of your assignment. Keep it simple and stick to the essentials. You will save yourself a lot of work.

- Start by getting organized. Make up files: a storage file, an insurance file, a travel file, a health file, a school file and so on. That way, if you have to make inquiries or if you have to find a particular paper, you know at least where to start your search.
- Reduce your stress by double-checking all the instructions from the moving, storage and insurance companies. Make a note of all deadline dates. When in doubt, ask questions or you'll go through all of the paperwork again.
- Read the fine print on the customs forms. If you want to avoid the aggravation of more red tape and of extra

trips to the customs office, limit the amount of so-called trouble items. The list varies from country to country, but usually brand new items of almost any kind, electronic equipment, bicycles, motor bikes, sports equipment, products made of unfinished wood, liquor, guns, pistols and pornographic materials attract in-depth scrutiny by customs agents.

- Keep an eye out for your travel documents such as visa, passport and airline tickets. If they do not arrive at the promised time, call the company and inquire. Do not assume that all will be taken care of automatically.

My daughter and I were supposed to get on the plane on a Saturday. On Monday of that same week my visa had not arrived. A needed document was missing, but nobody had informed me. I found out about this from the responsible authorities in New York when I called them in a state of, should we say, bridled panic. Talk about stress!

- The more decisions you make with your partner ahead of time, the less pressure you experience, the longer you will ride the elation wave.

What Possessions Should Be Shipped?

The company will tell you what our allowed shipping weight is. It is up to your family to decide what should be taken along to your new home. Separate the inventory into different sections: what is shipped, what is stored, what is put into safekeeping and what is sold or given away. (See check list in back of book) You now have the opportunity to really clean out that attic and to hold the garage sale of the century.

The basic rule that applies to shipping is to limit the amount of clutter. Have each family member decide on his/her essentials and personal treasures that need to be packed. Review all chosen items and make a list. How many articles are sent? Are they relevant? Can you get by with less? Are they on the customs exclusion or trouble roster? Only what figures on the final 'approved' list goes, end of story. Don't allow a million changes because you will probably be left to take care of them.

Should your partner leave early, make sure that you hold his/her wish list in your hand. Try not to assume responsibility for the safety of highly revered, prized possessions. I did not let my husband leave until he made storage arrangements for his model railroad equipment and clarified shipping details for his pet computer. That was one of my smarter moves!

For insurance and customs purposes all articles have to be catalogued and assigned an approximate dollar value. Since this exercise is rather time consuming and cumbersome, you have to proceed strategically and start early. If I had waited with my sorting and deciding until my insurance forms arrived, I would have been in big trouble.

Put all the items that will be shipped into one room. Make piles: books, clothes, china etc. Usually the movers do the actual packing. Sorting your belongings takes a while and after a few days you will have almost forgotten what you all got lying around in those corners. Therefore, compile a list of the nature and number of items as you carry them into the to-be-sent room. Now you know exactly how many coats, vases and utensils you got.This will eliminate a lot of stress and frustration once you are faced with the official documents. You merely have to fill in the blanks and transcribe numbers.

Pack some pictures, books, music tapes, CDs or anything sentimental and important that keeps you connected to your homeland. The fact that you join the illustrious ranks of the expats does not mean that you forget about your roots. Subscribe to some magazines that will keep you informed about the gossip and the happenings at home.

Furniture usually goes into storage unless, of course, you decide to sell it before you leave. Among the effects that you ship you might want to include that extra comfortable chair or that special table if it gives you the down-home feeling that you'll crave especially in the beginning.

Before you fill entire crates with video tapes of favorite movies and of tender family moments, make sure that they are compatible with the television and VCR playback systems in your host country. Many expats have carried a lot of worthless weight because they neglected to check on such details. There are video stores that can convert your tapes into just about any format for a fee.

There is always a lot of confusion on the subject of electrical appliances. TVs, VCRs, microwaves, refrigerators and stereos are best rented on site. Check the customs regulations in regards to electrical and electronic equipment. Make sure that you do not end up paying import duty on shipped items.

Do you really need all those state-of-the-art kitchen toys? You might have to part with your beloved bread-maker or food processor for a while. Voltage and frequency differences in your new home will probably render them useless. Taking along a transformer does not even guarantee success. Appliances equipped with dual voltage are usually preferred. Don't forget adapter plugs though, and don't neglect to adjust the voltage switch, if any, before use.

Jennifer had not checked the details on her curling iron. Before it went up in smoke, it singed her hair down to the roots and gave her second degree scalp burns. The event marked her first medical emergency while on assignment.

Take a selection of favorite jewelry pieces only if such items are truly needed or even appropriate in your future location. Jewelry, heirlooms and important papers are best put into safekeeping.

A note on excess baggage.
We all agreed in our group that we sent way too much.

- Half of my clothes were too heavy and did not fit into the color scheme of our area. The Salvation Army did not even have much use for them. I should have given them away or stored them before I left!
- Also, I brought way too much china. Then again, I did better than the poor soul who packed three sets of dishes, including her Limoges. Most likely, you will not be giving formal dinners. Simply take your everyday plates, cups, glasses and cutlery. Should you have a barbecue for the masses, you will probably use paper plates anyway. Other expats also bring their own dishes if you ask them to. Large business functions are usually organized at a hotel or at a similar venue.
- Hubby does not need the electric drill and all sorts of tools. Hopefully he will not have to build a house or a car from scratch. If things break in your rented home, the landlord will have to take care of the repairs. Again take the essentials—hammer, pliers, screwdriver—for hanging pictures or for doing some easy emergency work.
- Any motorized equipment is best left at home. Leaf blowers, mowers and chain saws just weigh you down. One expat shipped his motorcycle. I will not even begin to tell this tale of red tape! We all thought that he might not live long enough to see the thing clear customs. Once it was released, he had lost his taste for riding it. Of course, he'll still have to send it back home again!
- When bringing books limit yourself to the truly important ones. We shipped plenty and bought more while on site. We ended up having a pretty good library in town and could have saved ourselves some weight.

- Give each child a box to fill with must-have toys. Kids tend to take every game they ever owned, every stuffed animal and entire 5000-piece Lego sets. You have to set limits and enforce them.
- Think twice before you ship the home-gym and all sorts of sports equipment. These items add a lot of weight and often attract the eyes of suspicious custom agents.

Even though Jerry was transferred to the tropics, he sent his whole ski outfit. Who knows? Maybe one of those days he would hit the slopes in New Zealand. The suit is growing mold somewhere in a box in his garage. He forgot all about winter adventures because now he snorkels and dives in the South Pacific.

Nan stood her ground and brought her treadmill. She has been unable to solve the electrical problems and so it will be shipped back—unused. Nan joined a gym which got her in contact with other expats as well as with some local people. She enjoys that a lot better than working up a sweat all by herself in her living room.

- Carpets, and rugs add a lot of weight and might not fit into the scheme of your new dwelling. It happened to me! The rug that I shipped never even got unpacked. The color, the fabric and the measurements were all wrong. Hopefully, it will survive the heat and the humidity as it lies in the corner of the spare bedroom.
- Drapes and blinds! Window treatments are best bought on site.
- Store paintings and major works of art. That way you do not risk losing them or having them stolen or damaged. Maybe a good friend or a relative will watch those treasures for you.
- Evaluate the need for all that bulky hobby equipment. Easels, weaving looms, pottery wheels, whole sets of model railroads and sculpture tools will probably not

be needed. This of course all depends on the individual. Maybe you have a way of carrying on with your crafts. Sometimes it is difficult to get the correct materials such as paints, clays and molds on site. So make sure that you have a way of providing these essentials before you ship a lot of worthless weight. Some expats have discovered the beauty of local or native crafts. Could it be time to learn something new?

- So that departing expats do not even think about shipping the old sedan, most companies have cars on the top of their exclusion list. The usual rule is that whoever insists on taking the car, picks up the tab for the transfer and customs costs. But what should one do with the family car?

During our first year I tried to hang on to my beloved Grand Am. I thought of having a friend drive it now and then, but I dismissed the idea because I would have worried about accidents and liabilities. So it was left to accumulate dust in the garage. On our first trip back it got sold!

Cars like to run, to be useful. Sitting in a shed or under a tarp somewhere in the yard is not good for them. The seals dry out and leak, the battery dies, the engine gums up, the tires become square. Give your car another chance at a productive life by finding a loving new owner.

Getting Prepared Healthwise

Now is as good a time as any to look at the various health issues that need to be considered in anticipation of your move.

As you prepare for visa health formalities you might as well collect some of those very handy and often very important documents that could help you out in a case of an emergency while overseas.

- Get a letter from your doctor reviewing the state of each family member's health, outlining problems, allergies and current treatments. If you ever had an electrocardiogram (EKG or ECG) done, take a copy along. If not, ask your physician about doing at least a baseline EKG before you leave. It serves as comparison should the need ever arise to check on the heart while overseas. This is not only important for men but also for women, especially after menopause.
- Ask the pharmacist to provide you with a complete list of the names (generic and trade names), dosages, purpose and instructions of all of your medications.
- Have all documents translated and transcribed into the language and alphabet of the country where you will live. Check the Yellow Pages for language specialists and translators. Sometimes this service is included in the expat package. University language departments have been of help to me in the past.
- Find out how much medicine for personal use you are allowed to bring into the country. Ideally, it should last until your next home visit unless you can get the same product overseas.
- Can you have medication mailed to you? Consult your local Post Office for details. Also check on the laws of your host country ahead of time with the embassy. Leave a copy of the rules and instructions with your pharmacist.

Especially with the illicit drug trade going strong, countries have usually strict guidelines regarding the mailing of chemicals. Secure the proper permits. It is very stressful to be interrogated and to be put in handcuffs due to unlawful import of 'waterpills'!

- Get all your prescriptions filled before you leave. Have the pharmacist put the expiration date on the vials.

That way you have at least some idea of the possible shelf life of your medicines.

Hot and humid weather makes medicine expire faster than the date printed on the bottle. Even though I stored my medications as best I could, some of the products literally decomposed in the original, closed and sealed vial. Always inspect your medication before taking it. Don't take any tablets that have changed color, that look puckered or that smell differently from what you remember.

- Is the medicine that you take available in your prospective host country? What suitable alternative is available? Your pharmacist can already help you with some of these challenges, otherwise the folks at the embassy might be able to check with their local pharmaceutical board. This type of information can help in case of an emergency, such as losing medication or running out. Incidentally, never put your medicine in your checked luggage. Always keep it with you as carry-on.
- Take a first aid course if you got time. Be as self-reliant as possible. If you go to a tropical country, know how to handle snake bites. This is especially important if you will live in a remote area.
- Learn about dangerous and poisonous critters, pests and reptiles in your area. Know which hospital or clinic carries antivenins.
- Get a dental and eye check before leaving home.
- Invest in a spare set of glasses or contact lenses and don't leave the sunglasses behind. For more information on sunglasses, refer to "Avoiding Damage from Sun" in the section on "Health Overseas."
- Do you know what your blood group is? There is no better time to find out.
- Get all immunizations up to date and carry a copy of your immunization record.

- Ask your pharmacist what type of medicines you should include in your home emergency kit. (See check list in back of book) Discuss possible drug interactions between your prescription medicines and those that you will purchase over-the-counter. Clarify all children's dosages.

The products that one uses the most for self-treatment are those for minor aches and pains, colds, allergies, wound care and digestive problems. Don't forget scissors, tweezers and a thermometer. Include some water purification tablets especially if you will live and travel in tropical climates.

Some companies have ready-made emergency kits for their expats. Make sure that you know what all of the products are, what they are for and how and when to use them. Are they indicated for all family members?

Especially when sending people to more remote areas, companies often include a sealed pouch with disposable syringes, needles and skin wipes. That way the employee has a clean supply should there be a need for an injection.

- Discuss the specific, current treatments for travelers' diarrhea in your area with your doctor or pharmacist. Obtain some instructions for preventing dehydration and for replacing lost minerals and salts or electrolytes.
- A prescription for a mild sleeping pill has helped many an expat take a bite out of the much dreaded jet lag. Discuss this with your physician. The active ingredients in most over-the-counter sleep aids are antihistamines. Their effects usually last too long and make most people too groggy in order to qualify as good travel choices.

Don't rely on magic jet lag cures such as Melatonin and other fads. The best way to fight the misery is to get enough sleep before you leave. Eat light a few days before departure, on the actual day of travel and while you are in the air. Even though airline fare is becoming more heart-friendly, it still contains its share of fat and salt. Also, it is uncomfortable to sit in a crunched position with a tummy full of food that is hard to digest. There is no law that dictates that you have to eat everything that is put in front of you.

Avoid or minimize caffeine intake. Stay away from fat, salt, heavy spices and from loads of dairy products. Most of all don't drink alcohol when flying. It irritates the stomach, and it dehydrates.

As soon as you know what time it is at your destination, reset your watch. This will help your mind adjust more easily to time differences.

- While overseas you will discover that some commonly available toiletries and comfort medications can be hard to find. If you use a particular brand of makeup or skin care products, buy a good supply before heading out. Chances are that you will find the same kind overseas, but if not, you are prepared.

If you depend on a lot of homeopathic and other alternative medicine products, pretend that they will not be easy to locate.

Paper products such as Kleenex, toilet paper and feminine hygiene items are almost nonexistent in some places. I could never get any decent sugarless throat lozenges where we lived. Toothpaste for sensitive teeth or with tartar control and special contact lens products are some of those elusive luxury items that you might like to stockpile until you learn which products you can buy in your host country and which ones you have to import.

So, sit down and make a list of your family needs for general health maintenance. Get started early because all of these preparations take time and weeks fly!

Immunizations and Disease

Afflictions due to poor hygiene and disease-carrying mosquitoes, viruses and all sorts of bugs have a way of spoiling trips and expat assignments. Incidentally, whenever illness follows a trip, mention your travel route to your doctor. It could save you a lot of aggravation and bring into focus a maybe not so obvious diagnosis.

A lady who had been a missionary in Africa went to the dermatologist because she had a white, discolored spot on her hand that proved numb to the touch. The fact that she mentioned where she had spent some considerable time pointed the doctor in the right direction. The spot was the first manifestation of leprosy. Treating her condition was not an issue. Making the correct diagnosis was crucial.

Immunizations have done such a marvelous job of protecting us from some of the most debilitating diseases. Yet, now and then they fail to produce the desired results. There are also those afflictions for which a vaccine is not available. When dealing with disease in general, the very simple and proven motto remains that an ounce of prevention is so much better than ten pounds of cure. Sometimes, depending on what we catch, there might not be a cure. That is a nasty thought.

In order to keep yourself healthy while on expat tour:

- Find out about the health risks in your area.
- If a vaccine is available and if it is not contraindicated in your case, get it.
- Don't think that immunizations will protect you 100%.
- Avoiding the risk factors is often the best way to avoid disease.

What types of medicines and shots you need depends on your future location and on your current vaccination status.

Discuss these topics with your doctor. Recommendations keep changing since organisms tend to develop resistance to treatment, mutate, migrate and sometimes, if we are lucky, become extinct. Progress is continuous in this very dynamic field of disease prevention. Many vaccinations that were given only by injection are now available in oral tablet or liquid form.

Information updates are continuously published by institutions like the World Health Organization (WHO) and the Centers for Disease Control (CDC) in Atlanta. CDC has a 24 hour Traveler's Hotline. The U.S. Public Health Service has been of great help to me.

I refrain from bombarding you with lengthy charts and confusing maps since it is obvious that all of that tedious work might be obsolete by the time I would finish. Suffice it to say that, in order to avoid unpleasant surprises, you need the latest data and information.

Start on your fact-finding mission with one of the knowledgeable agencies. Find some information on the specific health problems in your area and don't panic. Forewarned is forearmed. You will not just be a tourist. Your own living quarters and cooking facilities give you much better control over the family's quality of life and overall health. By using plain old common sense, a lot of the curses can be successfully dodged. Let me repeat once more one of the golden rules of health: the most effective way—and sometimes the only way—to escape disease is to avoid the risk factors.

Chances are that your company has done at least some of the health and immunization investigations for you, but don't count on it. Nobody even asked us if our tetanus boosters were up to date!

Think for yourself because there is a lot at stake. Some preventive treatments have to start weeks or months before you leave. More importantly, do not let yourself get discouraged by human resource people who tell you that you over-react. In the end, they are not on their way to Borneo or to Katmandu, you and your family are.

Never go on assignment without having checked yourself on the immunizations required to protect yourself and your family from disabling and potentially fatal disease

I am still in shock at the mere thought of the executive who went on a lengthy business trip to India and to Pakistan without even inquiring what health problems might topple him. He assumed that the people who made the arrange-ments had checked on the necessary precautions. Of course, he got quite sick and was attended by a local doctor. He was lucky to get some help. What type of bug he caught, what medication he swallowed, we rather not think about. He did come back, barely in one piece. The whole drama could have been prevented with a pre-emptive thought. Never assume that anybody did this kind of thinking for you unless you have ample proof to the contrary.

As I mentioned in the beginning, many of the medical and general health concerns depend on where your assign-ment will take you. If you go to a western, industrialized country you should have few worries, especially if all your routine immunizations and boosters are up to date.

The usual vaccinations of mumps, measles, rubella, diph-theria, pertussis, polio and tetanus go a long way. Discuss your immunization status with your physician. Should you get boosters before you leave?

The main trauma arises when your transfer takes you into less developed or remote areas where hygiene is a problem. Hot, humid, tropical locations are particularly notorious for making the weary traveler or unsuspecting expat sick. We all take clean water and reliable food supplies for granted. But in many places around the world these so-called basics are not part of the everyday picture.

Whenever we have hygiene problems, we have to think of digestive complications such as travelers' diarrhea, dysentery, (diarrhea accompanied by fever and pus and/or blood in the stool) hepatitis, cholera, typhoid and various miseries resulting from the invasion of small or even microscopic worms and flukes.

Until you are thoroughly familiar with your area, until you know what is safe to eat in restaurants and on buffets, until you have developed a certain resistance to the microbial lowlife that surrounds you, take extra precautions.

Most diseases facing expats or travelers are related to poor hygiene and are caught through contaminated food and drink. We might think that most of these disorders are no longer a problem in our sophisticated world but they keep popping up with often disastrous consequences.

If a vaccination is available against the illnesses that plague your prospective location, discuss the case with your doctor. The usual way to proceed is to get vaccinated unless there are contraindications in your situation. (ex: pregnancy, other medical conditions, allergies against the vaccine and so on.)

I'll give a short listing of some of the infectious diseases that should be of concern to travelers as well as to those preparing for an expatriate assignment. As I mentioned before, the areas afflicted and the guidelines for prevention and treatment keep changing. Get the latest information well before you leave.

Cholera

Cholera is one of those disorders that hits the digestive tract. It is caused by agents called vibrios, most often by Vibrio cholerae. It is a health risk in areas of Latin America, Africa,

Asia and the Middle East. However, the Gulf Coast of the U.S. also reports cases now and then. The incubation period is 1 to 3 days. Cholera can be as mild as a case of diarrhea or it can be a severe, life threatening disease.

Cholera is spread by contaminated water and food. Vomiting and sudden, copious watery stools can put the patient at serious risk because of massive dehydration. Fluids and minerals have to be replaced in the same amount as they are lost. Prompt treatment with good hydration has lowered the mortality rate drastically to less than 1%. A vaccine is available but it has a high failure rate. Only 25 to 50% of those vaccinated are protected for 3 to 6 months against the disease. Some practitioners consider the vaccine of limited value because of such unreliable results and thus do not recommend it.

The best way to avoid cholera is to be cautious and to use common sense: don't drink the water unless it has been thoroughly boiled or unless it is bottled, and don't eat raw foods of any kind. Peel fruits yourself and practice good hygiene.

Your doctor might suggest that you carry an antibiotic with you, just in case. Be sure to get the instructions right on when and how to use it.

Typhoid Fever

Caused by the bacteria Salmonella typhi, typhoid fever is one more of those conditions passed along through contaminated food and drink, especially water. Typhoid fever can be very serious. The incubation period is around 8 to 14 days.

In the beginning the patient complains of general body pains, headache, sore throat, constipation and abdominal pain. A fever will develop and rise in stepladder fashion. If the disease progresses, intestinal lesions occur. Constipation is followed by 'pea soup,' sometimes bloody diarrhea. A rose spot rash, located mainly on the trunk, appears during the second week of illness in about 10% of patients.

Complications from full-blown, untreated typhoid include such things as intestinal hemorrhage, bowel perforation, pneumonia and hepatitis.

An oral and an injectable vaccine are available. If you are sent to a high-risk area and if there are no contraindications in your case, it is probably worth getting it. The oral form seems to be as effective as the injection and has fewer side effects. Even those people who are vaccinated should not expect miracles. Avoid the risk factors, namely raw foods and unsafe drink. Peel all fruits yourself. Make sure that all bottled water has an intact seal.

Traveler's Diarrhea

Besides contaminated food and drink this miserable condition can be precipitated by excessive fatigue, changes in climate, unfamiliar spices and foods, viruses and changes in the population of the bacteria which inhabit the bowel. Taking preventive antibiotics and all sorts of other medications is no longer recommended by most practitioners since treatment, if necessary, has to be targeted at the specific organism. Some people can have more problems from the plethora of chemicals that they swallow than they would have otherwise.

In the case of traveler's diarrhea, abdominal cramps, nausea, diarrhea, occasional vomiting but rarely a fever let the person know that there is trouble in bowel-land. With rest and fluid replacement the condition usually goes away by itself. But how does one distinguish traveler's diarrhea from more serious conditions or even from food poisoning? That becomes a problem for the expat or traveler who is left to rely on self-diagnosis.

Which agent causes a particular digestive problem can only be determined through blood and stool cultures or smears. This is why it is so important to discuss signs and symptoms of the various ailments with your doctor and to develop a treatment strategy ahead of time.

So, let me say it once more: The best approach to protection is to AVOID THE RISK FACTORS. Therefore, cook it, peel it yourself, drink bottled or boiled water, leave lukewarm and raw foods alone. When in doubt, assume the worst and don't touch it!

Especially if the job location is in isolated areas with limited or no access to medical care, physicians sometimes give their expat patients a supply of broad spectrum antibiotics. Once again be sure that you get clear instructions when and how to use them should diarrhea sour the overseas adventure. Familiarize yourself with the symptoms of the various diseases that hit the digestive tract and follow the prescribed guidelines carefully. Indiscriminate use of antibiotics can do more harm than good. As we have seen the medication has to be adapted to the bugs and to the region where you will live. Since many different agents can cause the same symptoms, it is important to have the condition diagnosed by a doctor if possible, especially if the home treatments fail.

Remember that prevention of dehydration is an essential first aid measure in all cases of diarrhea, no matter what the cause.

Hepatitis

How can we talk about disease resulting from poor hygiene without mentioning the group of viral disorders known as Hepatitis?

Hepatitis A, B and C are the conditions that we are most familiar with, but they are not the only types of hepatitis. We are zipping down the letters of the alphabet pretty fast! Since the various types of hepatitis are caused by viruses, antibiotics are not effective. The best way to avoid this miserable and potentially lethal condition is to once more avoid the risk factors and to get vaccinated if possible.

Hepatitis A is mostly transmitted through food handled by the unwashed hands of an infected person, through contaminated water and also through direct contact with an infected person. Raw seafood, such as oysters raised in contaminated waters, have spread whole epidemics of Hepatitis A.

Hepatitis B is usually caught through sexual contact with an infected person, through transfusion of contaminated blood products, through sharing of contaminated needles or through using contaminated medical instruments, acupuncture and tattooing tools.

Prophylactic injections of immunoglobulin have been used for years to protect temporarily against hepatitis. Since there are now vaccines available against both hepatitis A and B, it might be wise for you to be vaccinated before you leave. Expats need the best protection they can get. Ask your doctor about his/her thoughts on the subject.

Since the hepatitis list keeps growing don't assume that you are entirely safe because you are immunized against some of the viruses. Widespread intravenous drug use and the emergence of diseases resulting from a suppressed immune system have brought us an explosion of viruses which fancy liver tissue. Avoiding the risk factors is once more a wonderful way of avoiding the disease.

Hepatitis C is transmitted via unclean needles in drug users, contaminated blood products, and possibly also through intimate contact with an infected person. Unclean utensils used in body-piercing and tattooing have also been suspected. Hepatitis C can lead to serious liver damage, chronic liver infection and liver cancer.

No vaccine is available so far since the virus is an expert at mutation. Trials of treatment with Interferon seem to have some effect in younger patients and in those who have remained free of cirrhosis. Again, the best advice is to prevent the condition by avoiding the risk factors.

Malaria

Areas of Asia, Africa, South America, the eastern Mediterranean as well as numerous islands of the Pacific all figure on the map which outlines malaria risk zones. Incidents of malaria are on the rise.

Malaria is a serious tropical disease which can be fatal. It is caused by an organism called a protozoa and is transmitted to humans through mosquito bites. Since in many places the protozoa have become resistant to previously used medications, the type of medicine that will help protect you must be tailored to the organism in your area. Transmission of the disease often depends on the seasons and even on the altitude at which one lives. Malaria watches are on continuously, so it pays to find the latest information on prevention and treatment.

When my expat friend Linda traveled to Africa, she stated that she would be there for only a couple of days. Therefore she would taken 'precautions' and skip the medications. Maybe her blood is not as sweet as mine, but mosquitoes just love me. If I fail to spray one speck of exposed skin, they find it. Consequently, I would not even think of just taking precautions. It does not take days to catch malaria. One exposure to an infected mosquito is enough.

Beside prophylactic medication though, there are however some common sense preventive measures that are highly recommended: wear light colored clothing, use insect repellent, sleep under netting, keep the window and door screens intact, wear long-sleeved shirts and long trousers, avoid perfumes and colognes, stay indoors at dusk when mosquitoes are most active. If you can tolerate it, burn some citronella candles or mosquito repellent coils in and around the house. A vaccine against malaria has been discussed but is still in the very early stages at best.

When anti-malaria medicine is prescribed, find out if there might be drug interactions with your regular medications. Make sure that you understand the directions for use.

I once read about a gentleman who was admitted to the hospital in shock and who suffered cardiac arrest because he took his anti-malaria tablet once a day instead of once a week. He misread the label and could not understand why he was issued so few tablets!!

Outside of the tropics the diagnosis of malaria is often delayed and sometimes entirely missed. Physicians simply do not have enough experience with the symptoms. After catching the disease in a tropical paradise, a patient might come home complaining of periods of chills, sweating, nausea, headache and high fever. But who thinks along the lines of malaria when the snow flies outside and when the temperature has dipped to twenty degrees below zero?

Dengue Fever
So far there is no vaccine for this viral disease which is also spread by mosquitoes. The incubation period is usually 5 to 8 days. The patient comes down with a sudden very high temperature, severe aching, a sore throat and a measles-like rash. There is a chance to recover at this point unless the disorder turns ugly with severe bleeding into the skin, bleeding from the nose, mouth and intestinal tract. This is the highly dangerous hemorrhagic dengue fever which can kill the victim relatively fast.

The mosquito that spreads the affliction breeds in stagnant, usually filthy water and puddles, damp garbage piles, open sewers etc. In 1996 a severe outbreak of dengue fever in India made the headlines, but Malaysia, Indonesia, the Philippines and even Singapore reported cases. Heavy monsoon rains usually raise the risk of a major epidemic. How serious the consequences of such an outbreak are depends a lot on how fast the authorities and the people of the country react with insecticide spraying and general cleanup efforts. The best protection is good sanitation, the use of insect repellents and mosquito nets. Better yet, avoid high-risk areas.

Ross River Fever

This condition is caused by a virus and spread by mosquitoes. It is quite prevalent in Queensland, Australia, but can also be contracted in other areas of the country. The patient becomes very fatigued and often complains of arthritis-like pains which can be quite debilitating. A blood test is available to confirm the condition, but so far there is no vaccine and no cure. It can take months to recuperate. Some patients have ended up in wheelchairs. As of 1997 researchers in Australia are in the beginning stages of developing a vaccine. Hopefully it will turn out to be safe and effective so that it can be released in the next few years.

Yellow Fever

Transmitted through mosquito bites, this is a very nasty viral disorder which can have the sufferer knocking prematurely at the Pearly Gates. Yellow fever poses a risk in tropical and subtropical areas of South and Central America and Africa. Just about every country in the world asks for a yellow fever vaccination certificate as a condition for entry from those who have visited high risk places. Anyone without a certificate is not only denied admission but also faces possible quarantine.

The incubation period for yellow fever is 3 to 6 days. The disease comes on suddenly with high fever. There is both a mild and a severe form of the condition. In the mild form, which lasts from 1 to 3 days, the patient complains usually of headache, nausea, muscle pains and at times intolerance to light. The severe form turns rather gruesome with bleeding from just about everywhere, jaundice, 'coffee-ground' vomiting, severe pains throughout the body. Delirium, convulsions and coma herald a possibly catastrophic outcome

There is a vaccine available but it is only distributed to and administered by sites that are designated and approved by the World Health Organization. Only these sites can issue a valid Yellow Fever vaccination certificate.

If you are assigned to a Yellow Fever zone, the message seems clear to me: get vaccinated and stock up on mosquito nets and on appropriate mosquito repellents. Check on the latest recommendations. If there are severe contraindications to such a vaccination this—in my mind at least—would be reason enough to turn down an assignment in that particular area.

When discussing the questions of immunizations and preventive medications FEMALES should mention their status regarding pregnancy and birth control. Some medicines can interfere with the action of birth control pills, some are not recommended for pregnant women. Certain vaccinations should be avoided if possible early in pregnancy but are O.K. to give in the later stages. You will be routinely asked about such concerns. Just in case that you are not, keep these details in mind.

When you inquire about vaccination recommendations and contraindications ask the correct source. As stated earlier, the best agencies are the Center for Disease Control, the Public Health service and the World Health Organization.

A lady, who was about to travel to an Asian country, raised the eyebrows of her travel agent with the statement that she had called the country's embassy for advice on immunizations and that she was told that none were required.

I do believe that this is a classic case of crossed wires. From their point of view the embassy people were correct: no special certificates were required for entry into their country. They essentially said that she posed no hazard to their place. The woman, however, wanted to know what vaccinations she should get in order to protect herself from diseases in that particular location. She tried to find out from the locals what conditions were the flavors of the season at her travel destination.

This type of misunderstanding could very well be due to a language barrier problem. Then again, maybe her question was simply side-stepped by some worker who did not want to discourage tourist money.

Illness in a foreign country is no fun even under the best of circumstances. Before you embark on the big expat adventure, thoroughly investigate all health issues as they relate to your family and to the assignment. Get the vaccination story from a knowledgeable source and brush up on common sense hygiene precautions. Since the pound of cure is often difficult to find or even nonexistent, an ounce of prevention is definitely the best strategy.

Pre-departure Financial Concerns

Now that you have thought and obsessed about the preparations for the big move and about health details of all kinds, step back for a moment and turn your attention to some pre-departure financial matters.

A friend of mine sold some stocks while he was living overseas. He was taxed on the gains both at home and in his host country.

Do you anticipate any major financial moves while you are away on assignment? If so, discuss the possible consequences with your finance specialist or get some answers ahead of time from the tax office.

- If you plan on selling any assets such as property, stocks or bonds that will be subject to Capital Gains taxes, might it be better to sell them BEFORE you leave? If you sell them while you are living abroad, you might end up, as my friend did, paying taxes on your profits in your host country as well as in the U.S.

- If you plan on selling your house before you leave, have you had any nibbles or firm offers yet? What happens if the sale goes through while you are already abroad?

The U.S. allows an exemption on Capital Gains on the sale of your primary residence if you are on an overseas assignment and purchase another home within four years of the original sale. If you are not sure about any of these issues, it is best to check with the professionals before running into some nasty surprises.

- If you keep your house: did you file for non-homestead property status with the appropriate agency? Did you notify your insurance agent that you, the owner, will not occupy the premises ?
- Take along a copy of your previous year's tax returns. When the time came for filing our taxes, we had to fill out all the preliminary information to send into the tax advisor's office. Many of the details came from the previous year's statement.
- Be sure that address changes have been sent to all financial institutions: banks, credit unions, financial consultants, credit card companies, insurance companies and so on.
- I took some U.S. checks with me. Bills still came in from home and this made it easier to pay them. I preferred not to rely on family members to take care of these details. Make sure that the checks show your forwarding or mailing address. Ours was the address of the company office that dealt with our mail.
- Request monthly statements from all financial institu-

tions and advisors. It is simply easier to keep track of your accounts with regular, more frequent statements. Remember that you are far away from home. I tell you from experience that it can be costly to catch up on the latest status of your accounts through long distance calls. Buy yourself something nice with the money that you would spend in voice-mail-jail and on wasteful on-hold periods.

- Get non-toll-free numbers for each of your financial institutions. U.S. toll free 1-800 numbers may not be accessible from your foreign location. We were finally able to connect via our long distance discount company.
- Pay off your bills before you leave, if at all possible. There will almost certainly be a delay before you get your first mail once you are overseas. Start with a clean slate.

Last Minute Details

Congratulations! You have almost made it! It is time to sit back and to go through the last check list: (also see back of book)

- Do you have all your necessary important papers such as school transcripts, employer letters of recommendation, copies of insurance policies, receipts for tax purposes and so on?
- Do you have your airline tickets, travel itinerary, in-date passport and visa?
- Did you notify the electrical, gas and telephone companies of your move?
- Did you mail all those change of address cards? (see checklist for help)
- Did you buy those treats that your family will not want to miss, especially in the beginning?

It might be a good time to stock up on macaroni and cheese, candy, canned pumpkin and popcorn to only name a few? Note that sugarless and low fat items will probably be hard to find overseas unless you will live in a major city. In many cultures these products are not high on the priority list. Check which items you are allowed to ship to your location. Regulations can be pretty strict. Commercially packaged foods are usually fine. Aunt Margaret's super-duper fruit cake will have to wait until you are back on leave.

- Has every family member seen the dentist and the eye doctor if needed? Physicals are probably already completed due to visa regulations.
- Did you get all your prescriptions filled?
- Do you have all your health documents such as health history, copies of special tests and so on?
- Are all immunizations complete?
- Did you secure a duplicate set of glasses or of contact lenses for all needy family members? Did you pack the UV protecting sunglasses?
- Have you met your property manager yet?
- Did you bring documents, heirlooms, unneeded credit cards, checks and jewelry into the safety deposit box at your bank?
- Did you make a will?

Since there are never any guarantees in life, be brave and make a will. This action, by itself, does not invite bad karma! Settle the fate of all of your earthly possessions, such as money, teddy bears, property and so on. Clarify the children's situation should anything happen to you. It will give you peace of mind. Either enlist the help of an attorney or at least have somebody with legal experience check the details for clarity and loopholes. Let your family know that a will exists and in whose care you left it.

- Give your power of attorney to a trusted family member just in case a problem or family emergency arises while you are away.

The closer the time comes when you turn your back on your 'old life,' the more aware you'll be that you face indeed a major change. Now that the paperwork is finished and that the last boxes are packed, what could be the reason for all those butterflies that suddenly zoom about in the pit of your stomach? Have you started to mourn what you leave behind or are you looking forward to the next chapter of the big adventure? You might experience some rather ambiguous feelings, but the apprehension and confusion of those last few weeks have not succeeded in suffocating your initial excitement and elation.

At some point though, the majority of expats, especially the spouses, are hit by the famous letdown effect. Standing in an empty house, transferring the pets to a different home or holding the final travel plans in one's hand, often bring forth the tears held back for so long by some extra doses of adrenaline. Yes, it is O.K. to cry, but take a moment and pat yourself on the back for a job well-done. All those challenges left you maybe a bit shaken, but they failed to toss you off that surfboard. You are in fine form. You'll leave Kansas for good . . . but only for a while!

The Doldrums— The Final Days

Over the last few weeks or months, you have packed and worried. You have been excited and apprehensive. All of the emotional surges that tossed you around have left you rather numb. By now the idea of a transfer to a different part of the world is no longer new. Your research and homework have brought you in such close contact with your host country that mentally you are probably already there. After surviving the preparations for the move, you are quite confident that you will be able to handle any challenges that come your way. You have become a veritable expert in crisis management. You accept the fact that change is inevitably part of the deal. You accept your decision to go on expat duty as a good one. You look forward to the future. You are at peace with yourself. You coast into the pre-departure doldrums as you begin to separate from your old life.

The last emotional challenge that you still face are the multitude of good-byes, cries and 'last suppers.' I felt that I had almost made the mental transition to my new life and refused to have my final days gobbled up by depressing emotional endurance tests. This was my time to relax, my time to let go!

Last Suppers

There will be plenty of 'last supper' invitations coming your way! These can trigger acute attacks of doubt and separation angst in the departing expat. Acquaintances and miscellaneous people to whom you have not talked in ages all want to take you out once more or have you over for a last picnic.

Of course it is important to say good-bye to friends and family but try to limit the drain that these experiences can put on you. Last suppers all too often become burdening wet blankets. You might find out on these occasions that you will be doing most of the talking because all are greedy for the latest details. This can be exhausting especially at a time when you need all your strength to help you cope with the challenges that lie ahead. Choose wisely with whom you spend the time that is left in your old home. Spend it with those people who are truly important to you. Limit the time wasted on the ones who are only out for the gossip. Stay close to those who wish you well and cheer you up.

Contrary to popular belief, you will not disappear off the

face of the earth. The probability that you see everybody again is quite high. Unforeseen events will occur whether you are at home or overseas. So keep things in perspective and do not let people get you down with negative talk and attitudes.

The hardest time of the whole experience is most often *before* you actually leave. There is so much to do, so much to say good-bye to. It is almost as if you packed life as you knew it into some box and put it away somewhere. Deep down inside you know that you will probably never go back to the employment situation that you are leaving. You sense that the odyssey that you are about to embark on is already changing you profoundly. This is indeed a very thrilling feeling!

Even the hardiest of spouses report that they went through some kind of down period where they mourned their losses: the loss of their job or career, the loss of their family and friends, the loss of the familiar surroundings, the loss of their identity in a way. Some experienced these feelings of loss before they left home. For others the mourning came after they reached the new land. A certain amount of grief over the phase of your life that lies behind you is a natural part of the process. But eventually you let go of the old and welcome the new. Focus on the opportunities that lie ahead! You have so much to look forward to, so much to be thankful for.

'Airport scenes'

The day has come to head for the plane. What a relief! If you can successfully dodge unnecessary and depressing 'airport scenes,' you save yourself a lot of grief.

After some frantic weeks filled with hard work and turmoil, you are finally on your way. Make sure that you pick only optimists to accompany you should you decide to take an entourage to see you off. You are probably tired, somewhat apprehensive and excited all at once. Leave people whom you suspect to become a burden at home.

Linda's poor parents fell apart right at the check-in counter. By the time she sank into her seat, Linda was so depressed and felt so guilty that she cried most of the way from Dallas to Rio! What a soggy start to the great adventure!

All my life I have detested so-called airports scenes. Usually, those who tag along attempt to be composed, at least in the beginning. Eventually, somebody starts the wailing process. He cries, you cry, she cries, everybody cries and hugs. If you cannot dig up any emotionally balanced companions, remember that a taxi takes you there without the trauma. The ride to the airport symbolizes the finalization of the transfer process. You should allow yourself to sit back, relax and enjoy the feeling. Stepping on the plane is actually quite a liberating experience. The frenzy has come to a close. No matter what comes your way, you are ready for it. You might even catch yourself thinking ahead, looking forward to the big adventure that is now only hours away. No matter how great the stresses of the last weeks or days have been, you are planted firmly on your surfboard, and the tourist within you is more alive than ever! You search for your brochures. You are up! You have begun to ride the wave of the globetrotter high.

IV

What Do I Do While I'm on Assignment?

The Globe-Trotter High

You arrive in your new country, probably at bit confused, maybe a tad apprehensive but certainly excited. You might have this ambiguous feeling of being merely a visitor who intends to stay for a while. There is so much to be experienced, so much to be learned. The feeling of elation that probably energizes you at this point is comparable to the elation that overcame you in the very beginning when you were told about your possible overseas posting. Time for a nautical check—look to see where you are on the 'wave chart.' Please see Figure #2.

I'll never forget our first day in Australia. We arrived in the hotel around 8 A.M. The sun was already so high in the sky that it felt like 3 P.M. I looked down into the street and thought: "Goodness, that's Australia down there! I am literally Down Under." The mere thought of being so displaced gave me the jitters. But it also kicked the tourist within me back into gear. I wanted to see this place. I was somewhat scared, but curious. I carried a list of all of the things that we

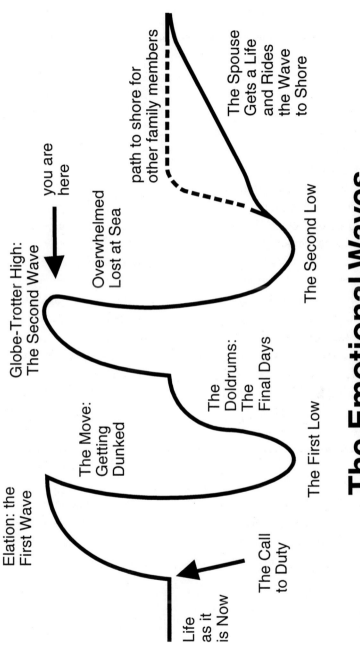

The Emotional Waves
Figure #2

should see and do as soon as we got off the plane. From the boat ride on the river to the sheep shearing show in the nature park, all the bases were covered. My husband tells me that during this initial arrival period we took almost half of our expat pictures. We went somewhere different every weekend. Just like those before us, we could not get enough of soaking up the brand new scenery, tastes, smells and experiences. Everything was different: the trees, the flowers, the birds. Even the night sky was different!

Most new expats that I met reported that they explored their new home in a most voracious way as soon as they arrived at their destination. Generally this was the first intimate contact that they had with their host country, and they used every spare minute to go and do something. While riding the wave of the globe-trotter high, expats tend to suffer from acute attacks of sensory overload. You will be the same way. You will also unpack your brochures and pamphlets before your toothbrush. Ride this wave of excitement and hang on to your surfboard because there are some rougher waters ahead.

Lost at Sea—Overwhelmed once More

While you make your first plans on what to see and do, don't forget about some of the more mundane but daunting functions that face you as a newly arrived exile.

If you do not know yet where you will live, chances are that you will start your tour in a temporary place such as a hotel or a furnished apartment. This of course means that one more move will come up fairly soon. Within 3 months we moved twice.

In order to get some normalcy back into life, make it your first project to find suitable accommodation. You are all together now and finding your dwelling should become a family affair. However, with the partner working, you, the spouse, will probably be in charge of the search team. Don't panic! Companies usually refer expats to local real estate agents or relocation consultants for help. Remember to look out for yourself though because you, the spouse and the children, will probably spend the most time at home. As I mentioned earlier, pick a place where you would like to live!

Besides hunting for a house, you might also want to find out what company will supply your furniture. Stop by for a look and check on prices. Stay within your allowance limits.

Setting the kids up in school and meeting the teachers is usually the next important project that brings a bit of reality back into life. Change is hard especially for children. Get ready for some early feelings of lonesomeness and of rejection.

Another assignment for the spouse is to do intensive 're-search' in the grocery stores. Finding the products that your family likes is important. Food becomes one of the early comfort measures. Especially in the beginning when there is so much change and upheaval you want to see and taste familiar things.

In our group the absence of Crisco shortening caused some major hardships. Baking just was not the same without it. So, anyone who went to the big city for a holiday knew what to bring: a can of Crisco from the local deli. It cost a fortune and the cans were tiny, but the bakers always cherished this very coveted gift.

Whenever you run across a familiar but unusual article in the grocery store, get it! Don't say: "I'll come back later for that." You might never see it again. We all went crazy when a store in our town got a shipment of low fat mozzarella cheese and of Sara Lee frozen bagels. It probably all happened by error. Since the stuff moved because we all bought it, the supply was replenished now and then. The fat free Angel

Food cake mix, however, never reappeared once the shelf was empty.

Yes, there is a lot to do, a lot to cope with. After an initial high many expats, especially the spouses, get thoroughly discouraged by what can look like insurmountable difficulties. Getting around in a strange place, coordinating the setup of the home, dealing with kids who might not like their school and hate the food, trouble with the new language and culture all boil together and overwhelm you again. Suddenly one misses everything that was left behind: the family, the friends, the old work place, the dog, the dentist and even the traffic jams. You drift around hugging your surfboard, lost at sea.

But it is a normal cycle: highs are followed by lows.

Ride the Wave to Shore

During this stage you begin to feel at home in your new country. You learn about the quirks of everyday living, and you pick up the pace of your new lifestyle. You settle in. Your surfboard is finally pointed towards the beacon that signals the shoreline.

By now you have already traveled a bit. You have found a place to live, and you explored the local shopping scene at length. You start to get used to your surroundings. Everyday life has begun. Gradually, groceries become less important. You almost do not miss the peanut butter anymore. Not finding, or not having Jell-O, is no longer be a major crisis. We all ended up doing just fine without all those specialty items that spoil us so much. You probably have already discovered some new and exciting tastes that threaten to rip you out of the old meat-and-potatoes rut.

Guess what! Your 'things' from home have just arrived. All the items that you packed, sorted and catalogued have to be unwrapped, unpacked and assigned a place in your new home. Yes! Think about the place where you now live as home. The faster you accept the idea, the better it is.

Anyway, for most expats life gets smoother once they receive their familiar things. The old frying pan, your trusted friend, has come to live with you again!! And look, there is Jeff's favorite pillow! Most pieces of your china survived the trip and, oh joy, need to be washed after spending weeks in clay paper and musty boxes.

Ironing wrinkled wear takes up a few days at least. Some people were born to be wild. Maybe you were born to press clothes? You'll start to wonder just as all of us have before you. Not to worry! The ironing phase passes, and then it is once again time to move on to other projects.

After cleaning and scrubbing the place from top to bottom you might want to tackle the window treatment situation. Most places do not have everything ready-made the way we are used to. The seamstresses and other creative persons are probably the only ones who enjoy this particular challenge.

The phone works! This is a great day for any expat because a link with the outside world is finally established.

As mentioned earlier, a move is a move. Basically, a lot of the chores and the preparations remain the same no matter where one ends up settling. Expatriates, however, are in the unique position of getting a good taste of how spoiled they all were in the homeland. So, you expect on-time deliveries, qualified help to be available for installations or fix-it jobs, accurate weather predictions, CNN, appointments to be kept, appliances to work properly . . . Wow, slow down, you are an expat now! Time to roll with the punches! Time to ride the waves!

Electricity and running water, both hot and cold, are luxuries that we all take for granted. As we have already seen, tap water, if it exists, often cannot be used without boiling it first. There are places where it takes years to get a telephone line. A useable toilet can be harder to find than the Holy Grail. I always felt that as long as I did not have to kill and clean my own chicken and fish, I could deal with the situation. Boy, was I a lucky lady!

A woman once told me that she was amazed at how different her host country looked once she lived there. She had been a tourist before. The meals were catered. She got pampered in resorts and was treated to some historical excursions that never took her past the open sewer that runs only a few blocks from the bus route.

Besides not-so-talented handymen, there can be some surprises of a different kind. Remember to cling to your surfboard.

So what? Nobody knows what wallpaper is, the elevator never works, you buy meat and potatoes on the black market, a spider the size of a hockey puck decorates the wall or a snake frolics in the backyard. The locals do not get upset at these things! So hold the tantrums! As an expat you have to learn how to handle those situations without losing too much of your dignity.

In the tropics I suddenly felt very fortunate that some competent pest exterminators were available. All those chemical-free-life philosophies went out the door when the first cockroach sped across the floor. Challenges and surprises are all part of the expat adventure! As you ride the wave, keep your patience and your sense of humor handy. Every now and then you need to fall back on them when an unforeseen event gives you a little test. No matter what your situation might be, don't lose your cool. You have been given the unique opportunity to learn about the rest of the world, a world that you'll start to see with different eyes. Hopefully, you'll emerge from this total immersion program a lot wiser and a lot more tolerant.

Now you see why it was so important to get yourself prepared and educated before going on assignment! A common complaint in the military is that the recruiter never said that it would be like this. Expatriates feel at times the same way. But don't worry! The less desirable aspects of expat life are balanced by the positive ones. In our case the tropical sunsets, the aromatic scent of woods and fruits, the coral cays, the fresh seafood and the 'no worries' lifestyle definitely outweighed the fact that there were some reptilian creepy crawlers around. They stayed out of my way, and I did not search for them. So, we were all happy! Once I had conquered my worse fear, namely to be confronted with a snake, I knew that I had adopted our new home.

As life calmed down around me, I felt that I was doing a great job settling in and heading towards shore. But like many other spouses I began to drift and to fall behind. My batteries were nearly empty, and an undefined need or void kept gnawing at me. I had to define a mission for myself, outside of the family.

How Is Your Family Doing?

Settling in your new home is a very busy time, especially for the spouse. It is easy to concentrate so much on living arrangements, furniture and plumbing details that you might forget to keep track of the various family members. They all need you in this period of enormous change. They need your patience, your wit, your advice. Step back for a moment and evaluate how widely open the communication channels are between all of you. Communication has been recognized as a major stress reducer and its power should not be underestimated.

How does your partner handle the job? Is he/she getting along fine with the new working partners and colleagues? Are the stress levels still under control or do contract negotiations and union problems take the wind out of his or her sail? Is it time to put life back into perspective over a nice cup of coffee or tea? You, the spouse, can help!

What do you hear from your children? During the first crucial months they need some extra hugs and words of reassurance. Often children surprise their parents by doing a lot better than anticipated. Yet, the parents should never underestimate the destabilizing effect that expatriate life can have on kids of any age. Be there for them should a time of crisis suddenly come about. Life in the new land will not only be a challenge for the adults. Encourage your children to talk to you and to share their experiences and impressions.

I learned a tremendous amount about our daughter during our own expat stint. We talked a lot more than we ever did back home. I had more time to spend with her since I was not sidetracked by a job and by all sorts of other duties. Our relationship greatly improved. I got a whole different outlook on teenagers' fragile egos. They might have us believe that they are hard as nails, but their soft core is ever so vulnerable. Breaking into social groups in new schools in an attempt to make new friends in a new land is a real anxiety churner. Incidents that would not have bothered her at her old school back home became major events while overseas.

Not being invited to a party brought on unexpected feelings of rejection. Being called 'a Yank' did not go over very well. But then New Zealanders were labeled as Kiwis and those of British background were referred to as Pohms. (prisoners of his or her majesty) And life goes on!

As parents we often forget how terribly important the social aspects of a teenager's life are. In order to overcome the much stressed isolation and acceptance factors, young people try to be cool and to fit in. This makes them very vulnerable to the temptations of drugs and alcohol and to put-downs by peers.

Again, any these problems can surface anywhere. I certainly know plenty of young people who have trouble without being on expat assignment! Living in a foreign land throws us off balance and merely tends to aggravate our shortcomings and insecurities, no matter how old we are. But, forewarned is forearmed. The important thing is to stay vigilant. Look for the little red flags that might signal depression and unhappiness in your child: not wanting to talk, unusual mood swings, overblown feelings of homesickness, too much time spent in isolation in his/her room, frequent crying, extreme snippiness or any other behavior that seems uncharacteristic for your youngster. Physical complaints such as frequent headaches, nausea or stomach problems may also point to the fact that there is trouble on the school and/or social scene. If a child sends you distress signals, it is time to investigate the case at once.

If your own emergency counseling does not seem to have an effect, don't let the situation get out of control by letting it drag on. Enlist the help of your expat liaison person at once in order to get professional advice on the matter. Companies are usually eager to assist you in any way possible. Unexpected problems with youngsters tend to sour expatriate assignments all too often unnecessarily.

Communicate with your children, now more than ever. Encourage them and boost their self-confidence at every chance you get. We should do that anyway as a normal part of parenting, but expat children need an extra dose of loving care. Incidentally, how youngsters react to their new situation depends a lot on the parents and on the preparation and support that they provide. Your attitude reflects on theirs. Chances are that if you, the parents, cope so will the children.

Your stay overseas is your chance to broaden your children's horizon. Keep teaching them about their new country. Talk to them about the cultural differences that might exist and help them understand. Children are often disturbed by extreme poverty. They cannot comprehend why boys and girls are not treated as equals. They do not take kindly to what they perceive as abuse of animals.

Whenever possible, take them with you when you travel, provided that you make the proper arrangements with the school. Forget about the macaroni and cheese! Encourage them to try different foods. Let them take part in activities that are unfamiliar and interesting to them: fishing, skiing, boating, sailing, bird watching, whatever. Motivate them positively. Make every effort to show them the fun and diverse aspects of expat life.

Eventually, time will heal all wounds, and the youngsters will settle in their new lives just as the adults will. Kids of all ages actually derive a sense of intense pride once they know that they have faced the challenge and mastered the art of living abroad. With a healthy dose of patience you will succeed in turning the overseas mission into a superb growing and eye-opening experience for the whole family. You will all happily ride that wave together.

Health Overseas

Keeping your family's mental attitude in check is important. It is, however, equally vital not to forget about their physical health. Depending on your location and on the travel that you will do, it is very important for you to know how to prevent damage from the sun and how to avoid digestive troubles brought on by breaches of basic hygiene rules.

Avoid damage from the sun!

Skin cancer alert!

Expatriate assignments into tropical climates seem to become more and more the norm. Business opportunities appear to be particularly numerous in the warmer areas of the globe. Especially if your tour of duty takes you to a sunny country, familiarize yourself thoroughly with the dangers of unprotected sun exposure.

Is there a hole in the ozone? Does it really matter? All we know for sure is that skin cancer of all kinds is on the rise just about anywhere in the world. Skin cancer kills!

Don't be fooled into thinking that a 'good tan' will ward off all evil. Let's face it: fair skinned people who got themselves a deep tan have put their hide through some major trauma to obtain the result. The lighter the skin tone, the more protection is indicated. Black people can even burn. The bottom line is that it is easier to be safe than sorry. Anybody should use sun protection tailored to their skin type.

"Slip, slop, slap" was the slogan of the Australian Cancer Fund. SLIP on clothing that protects your skin from the sun. Long-sleeve shirts and long pants should be considered if at all feasible. Ideally the fabric should be woven tightly enough so that it is not see-through. As clothes get wet the protection that they offer diminishes sharply.

SLOP on some sun protection lotion with an SPF of at least 15. These products must be applied 20 to 30 minutes before going outside. The chemicals need to penetrate the skin before they can do any good. Reapply every few hours just to be sure. Even so-called waterproof creams and lotions should be freshened occasionally.

Common places missed when slathering the stuff on are the ears, the back of the neck and the lips. Find some lipstick or lip-balm that also contains sun protectors. The top of the head is an other area that ends up blistered now and then. So before you leave the house SLAP on a hat. Baseball caps do not protect the ears or the back of the neck.

Never underestimate the power of reflected rays. Many an unsuspecting soul has gotten fried while 'protected' in the shade of a beach umbrella. Sand, cement and road coatings reflect so much UV that prolonged exposure can cause major injury. Be safe and put on sunscreen even though you wear a hat or walk with an umbrella.

Talk to your pharmacist about the medicines that you or your family members take. Do any of them sensitize the skin so that it burns faster and deeper? There is a long list of culprits that do just that. Some are worse than others, and it is important to be forewarned. Consistent common sense precautions should leave you with few worries.

Does every family member have a good pair of sunglasses? Sunglasses must protect the eyes from the damaging ultraviolet rays. They are not just a fashion statement. If the lenses are not properly coated with UV blocking chemicals, you run the risk of getting premature cataracts and burns on the cornea. The darkness of the glass is no indicator of the level of protection since UV blocking agents are mostly colorless. We have to rely on the manufacturer's label information. Glasses that are not labeled should not be bought. Also, the lenses have to be large enough to cover the eye and the sensitive skin around the eyes. If you squint while wearing your shades, the lenses need to be larger or darker, maybe both.

Some people are not scared by the possibility of getting cancer, but the threat of premature aging simply terrifies them. No matter what motivates you, there are plenty of good reasons to protect yourself and your family from the sun. As dermatologists keep telling us: if you want to keep a young, healthy skin, lead a shady life.

Avoid food poisoning!

Maybe you feel like you have a perfect knowledge of the hygiene precautions cited below. Read them anyway as a refresher. With every poor victim who experiences a digestive misadventure we get additional tips on how to avert trouble.

- Cooked food should be hot. Look for rising steam. Uncovered, lukewarm cuisine attracts flies and is a breeding ground for bacteria.
- Whenever I am on unfamiliar territory, I bypass so-called 'cold' dishes. Proper refrigeration is an art mastered by few. Beware of improperly refrigerated sandwiches, salads and baked goods with cream toppings.
- Water has to be boiled for at least five minutes before it can be considered safe. This might sound extreme but a 'good bubble' is not good enough. Some microbes can only be killed by prolonged exposure to high temperature. Use boiled water for brushing teeth and for rinsing the mouth. Remember that at high altitude water has a lower boiling point, so not all bugs might be killed. Use purification tablets if necessary.
- Until you find out how bad the situation is in your corner of the world, also use caution with high-water content vegetables and fruits such as cucumbers and water melons. Local growing patches are more than likely irrigated with contaminated water.
- Only drink bottled water if the seal of the bottle is intact and if the bottle is opened in front of you. Listen for the snap of the seal. Your water might have been 'bottled at the source' except not at the source that the Evian people had in mind.
- Clean off tops of bottles and cans with an alcohol wipe before drinking from them. You do not know who touched them and where they were stored before they appeared on the store shelf.

- Caution! Juice drinks are often reconstituted from concentrate with local water. Like dairy products, juices should be pasteurized and purchased in sealed containers.
- Forget about using ice in drinks unless you made it yourself from boiled water.
- Don't drink the milk or eat dairy products unless you see the word 'pasteurized' on the intact container. Drinking milk fresh from the cow might sound wholesome, but it is a big health risk unless it is boiled first.
- Beware of ice cream from unreliable sources. Again, one does not know if it was made from heat-treated milk or if the storage and dispensing equipment are sanitary. Listeria monocytogenes likes to live in unpasteurized dairy products and has been found to contaminate the tubes of ice cream machines. Boy, can that bug make a person ill!
- Stay away from raw or uncooked foods such as salads, vegetables and seafood. Especially seafood can be contaminated by helminths or worms. Sewage contaminated oysters have been responsible for outbreaks of hepatitis. Make it a point to avoid raw seafood even in areas where one normally trusts the integrity of the fare. While working in Europe, Glenn caught hepatitis from eating raw shellfish. During our stay in Australia a hepatitis epidemic was traced to raw oysters from a seafood farm.
- Avoid any food that is undercooked be that beef, poultry, seafood, vegetables or eggs. Salmonella, Campylobacter and E. coli are only some of the microbes that have a tendency to lead to a serious crisis in those afflicted.
- Avoid foods that are prepared with raw eggs: sauces such as Hollandaise and Béarnaise, dressings, mousse and mayonnaise.

In some countries it is almost impossible to get prepared sandwiches that are not smothered with either butter (pasteurized?) or mayo. This is often an unsuspected source of bacteria when people get violently ill.

- Until you know what you're doing, avoid street vendors, and take it easy on spicy ethnic foods. Spices and salsa do not kill bacteria.
- It can be unwise to assume that hotels and resorts are entirely safe. Usually they are. However, people who might be carriers of those illnesses that we have no immunity against can probably be found among the staff who prepare the food. No need to be paranoid. Simply keep this in mind. Don't let your guard down entirely and choose your foods wisely. Hands off the raw stuff and don't drink the water!!

Even at home I have witnessed some extremely poor hand-washing techniques from restaurant employees. It always makes me kind of weak when I see them disappear into the kitchen after a restroom stop where they merely passed their fingertips for two seconds under the cold water.

- Expats who lived in areas where it is a rule to hire local home help report that it is a good investment to watch out for those people's health also. Anybody with signs of diarrhea, suspicious cough, fever and skin disorders should be sent to a doctor. If your staff is ill, they can pass it on to you. Make the appointment, and pay the bill if necessary. It makes good health sense.

Finances Overseas

In the chapter on "Practical questions to ask the employer" I mentioned already two of the most popular financial questions that expats keep asking over and over.

- Is there an advantage to the spouse working for pay, and is it wise to invest in property overseas?

Hopefully you discussed the various options on these points with your tax consultant or with your financial advisor before you left. In our group, none of the spouses found that it was worth the aggravation to go job hunting. Tax problems and all sorts of technical difficulties curtailed our enthusiasm. We worked in our own way. We supported our partners and children. We tried to be active in the community, to learn from our experience abroad and to use some of the precious time bestowed upon us as an opportunity for personal growth.

I know of few people who got fancy with financial ventures. Those who tried wished that they had saved themselves the trouble and worry. But every case is different. Even though the prospects for spouse employment and for foreign investments might not look favorable at first, once you are on location you can certainly re-evaluate the situation.

One area that does become a bit of a problem is long distance credit card management. The mail is usually forwarded from the home office. With all of the different carriers involved delivery services tend to be plagued by glitches. This little quirk of expat life can cause some havoc with banking strategies. By the time we got our bills the accounts were either already overdue or the time left was cut so short that on-time payments became a problem. This can lead to bad credit ratings in a hurry.

In order to work around these problems some expats arranged for automatic bank pay from their account at home. Others called the various credit card offices towards the end of the billing period and sent in the payment for the amount due at that time. No matter which way you choose to arrange yourself, keep track of your statements.

In order to separate personal expenses from business expenses, use separate credit cards. This will eliminate the need for sorting through piles of statements trying to find the items chargeable to the company. The credit card people essentially do your accounting for you.

HUMOR BREAK
GET A LIFE!

It's five in the morning. I'm already up.

I sit and drink coffee. This is my third cup.
My husband still sleeps for he had a hard day.
My schedule is blank. Again, free to play!

Another lunch downtown with the gals!
By now we all sure are the closest of pals.
A few hours of gossip and of killing time,
of loitering in shops, not spending a dime.
As businessmen rush all staking their claims
I'm drifting about without any clear aims.

I've been over this town. I know every nook.
I've researched the stores to find things to cook.
I've studied the history, the old and the new
Who conquered and plundered, which army, which crew.
I have dusted and ironed garments galore.
These days "full of fun" are frankly a bore.

I miss the hospital, my friends—doctor Russ!
Why do I remember that ornery old cuss?
This means I'm in trouble. There is no doubt
I need something else to be thinking about.

The hospital pharmacy uptown, I do hear
needs a reliable and well-trained volunteer!
Since I've got that job, I am on a roll—
up to my kneecaps in quality control.
My days are bright now and meaningful too.
I contribute to mankind. I've got something to do.

Get a Life!

By now the children have started school, and the partner copes well with the new assignment. Your loved ones stand tall as they ride the wave to shore. You have done a great job of keeping all family members focused and communicating! But what about yourself? The waters seem to be smoothing out for everybody else, so why do you, the spouse, teeter on your surfboard? You can barely stand up, and you wonder if you will ever make it back to the beach. So close and yet so far!

You are tired of dusting and of doing laundry. Maybe the company provides you with hired housekeeping services. In certain countries hiring local personnel is almost a requirement. Others may think that you live like royalty, but you are no longer satisfied with looking out of the window! An idle day and a blank schedule are big enemies of the expat spouse. One can only shop so much and visit so many museums or art galleries!

Breaking-in periods can be particularly tedious if you live in a place where language barriers, both written and spoken, present serious stumbling blocks. If the smallest venture demands a gargantuan effort, it will not be long before you are discouraged. Therefore it pays to gain at least some elementary knowledge of your host country's language. Yet, no matter where one lives, getting used to a totally new environment, new customs, new foods and different ethnic settings can take the gusto out of anybody's life. The working partners often handle these low points with more poise because they have the stabilizing forces of job and colleagues to help them over the rounds. Nobody says that the adjustment period is easy for them. They also deal with different work ethics, different contracts and different equipment, but it is more difficult to wallow in misery when duty calls. Sometimes having to perform is good.

Jan, a laid-back, Lauren Bacall type lady, confided that shortly after she had arranged all the cabinets in her new home, she noticed an unusual tiredness about herself. The flurry of activity which surrounded the whole move had died down and so had she. She thought that she had trouble adjusting to the climate. Then she began to take naps in the middle of the day! She finally realized that boredom had hit in a major way.

Expressions such as restrained, locked-up and depressed are commonly used when expat spouses share their initial reactions to their new lives. After the globe-trotter high, another move and the settling-in period they admit that the days became longer and that the novelty of expat life began to wane. They report that feelings of lack of challenge and mission often put them into a foul mood at a time when they should have actually been very excited. Usually it is around this time that many spouses begin to contemplate what they have lost or given up. They think about home where they were in charge of their own lives, where they had their own jobs and activities, their own friends, their own money.

A rather unexpected revelation was that previously stable relationships appeared to show signs of strain. Partners who seemed to work very long hours, who attended more late meetings than usual and who even worked on weekends made spouses wonder why they relocated. Wouldn't it be easier and cheaper to spend time by themselves at home on their own turf? What rung did they actually occupy on their partners' priority ladder? Did the partner see the spouse in a different light now that he or she was a displaced person without clear goals? Obviously there were other people that were more pleasant or more interesting to hang out with.

With too much idle time on their hands some spouses truly inflated trivia and spun it into drama.

Do not fall prey to all sorts of suspicions that threaten to throw you off your surfboard! Your partner must also cope with tremendous change and turmoil. The higher the position of the working partner, the bigger the responsibility, the newer the business venture, the longer and the more unpredictable the hours will probably be for a while. There simply is too much to learn, too much to get used to!

If you feel, however, that the relationship with your partner is suffering, talk to him/her and fix it! Worrying serves no purpose! It is time to plan some activities together. Have a night or two away from the now familiar four walls. Go for supper or to the theater. Treat yourselves and do whatever you both enjoy. The job should not become all-consuming or there might be trouble around the bend.

Since the antidote for worries and boredom is action, it is very important at this point to become pro-active and to brainstorm on outside interests. Failing to do so will greatly delay your ride to shore. Find a new mission for yourself! Create your very own niche! GET A LIFE!

- Are there any educational programs that you might be interested in? Go ahead! Learn the language! Some spouses have increased their computer skills considerably while on assignment. They finally had the time to take a structured class on programs that they had sort of learned on the job back home.
- Are there any other expats or otherwise displaced persons in the area with whom you might get together now and then? Especially in bigger cities or in Third World countries expatriate groups tend to be well organized. If you love the arts, history, literature and so on, you might find some special interest groups that you can join. You find people with whom you have something in

common. You share your interests and hopefully some good laughs. You find out that your situation is not unique. Everybody else has at least some of the same problems. Talking and joking with peers is very cleansing at times. You might organize some excursions or attend seminars and lectures with your new cohorts.

It is important though not to let these meetings—especially the lunches—degenerate into whining sessions. You need to encourage each other. Constant complaining and belly-aching gets awfully old awfully fast.

While out and about, always use discretion. Loose lips are said to sink ships or let's say that they can cause a lot of trouble. There is no need to be paranoid, but watch what you say and to whom you say it. The other spouses might be linked to business partners or business competitors of yours. In order to stay out of trouble, make it your personal policy never to discuss company business at the lunch table. Also, local people might look towards you for some insider information on employment opportunities. I was asked repeatedly in the grocery store whether our company was hiring or not. Human resource departments handle those questions.

- Do you have any hobbies? Especially in the initial stages of the assignment, spouses are inclined to dive into those hobbies and activities that they never had time for. That's great! Take some time and spend it on yourself while you have the opportunity to do so.
- Some of the ladies in our group formed their own book club. They met regularly to discuss what they had read. It kept them busy and challenged. On top of that, they learned from each other.

Investigate the various clubs in your area. Talk to the local development board or read the Yellow Pages if there are any. Usually all interests are represented from quilting to model railroading or bird watching. If you live in a segregated society, the clubs might include only foreigners and other ex-pats, but you still have a chance to meet a lot of interesting people. If you have the opportunity to join a local group or club, grab it and meet the local population on neutral ground.

- Is there a gym that you might join? Some people love that. I always found it difficult to socialize dripping wet and out of breath. Besides, I keep falling out of step during aerobics. Too many feet! Gyms, however, teem with prospective running or jogging partners. If you are an athlete, give it a try. If you are not, try anyway. This might be your big chance to get in shape.

- Have you ever been a volunteer? Wonderful experience! In many countries expat spouses often cannot be gain-fully employed because of immigration restrictions, li-censing problems and visa limitations. This does not mean that you have to become idle. Define your inter-ests. Do you enjoy working with children, the poor, the elderly, the sick, the handicapped? Do you want to lend a hand in church, in the library, in the art gallery? Believe me, your skills and enthusiasm are desperately needed. Satisfaction is almost guaranteed! Nothing makes you feel better than knowing that you helped somebody simply because you wanted to.

Be honest though with your volunteer recruiter and let him/her know how much time you really have available. Since they do not get paid, volunteers tend to think that they can show up at their own whim.

Even though it is important to keep busy, it should be a meaningful busy. There should be a feeling of accomplish-ment. If you play your cards right, you might even be able to offer your services in an area similar to the job or specialty you had before becoming a professional spouse. In order to find contacts, ask your company, your neighbor, your pastor or, if it is an option, read the telephone book. The phone book is a totally underestimated well of information. Look for the service agencies, and you will never be bored again.

Before going on assignment with my husband, I was a hospital pharmacist in the U.S. After some time in our new country, the need to find a niche for myself made me call the local hospital. Were there any areas where they could use assistance? The medical superintendent recruited my services as a volunteer hospital pharmacist on the spot. I stayed in my field, and the pharmacists at the site were glad to see me coming since they did not have any extra money in their budget to hire some much needed help. After a while, I also wrote a weekly health column for the local paper, again on a volunteer, unpaid basis. The fact that my efforts were recognized by the community as a service was pay enough.

Volunteering has various advantages:

- it makes you feel good because you give of yourself to others,
- it gives you a feeling of accomplishment,
- it keeps you busy,
- it opens a door into your community,
- your services will benefit the community,
- you might learn a new skill or two,
- you gain a new understanding of the culture,
- it closes the gaping hole in your future resumes,
- it leaves you freedom for travel with your family.

- A lot of spouses use the opportunity of overseas assignments to learn some techniques in ethnic cooking. Using cookbook recipes is great, but perfecting the authentic flavors and textures is an art that can only be learned on site.

Go ahead! Dazzle your friends with that perfect brioche. Tease them with a to-die-for curry or satay. Keeping a

Schnitzel from tasting like leather can be a challenge. Chef Oskar will teach you a trick or two. Cooking is a fun and a creative activity that produces rewarding and delectable results. More people should try it!

- Got an idea of your own? Do you see some needs that are not met? Form a new club or group! Too much garbage in the neighborhood? Organize a cleanup! You might just leave your very own legacy.

It is no longer a secret that becoming active in the community is a high priority mission for an expat spouse. Through your work and presence you might be able to break down social barriers in a way that no managing course ever taught. What you learn out there in the trenches could be a tremendous resource for your partner and for the company. Again, never underestimate the importance of the spouse's role in the expat experience!

- While you are in that part of the world that has been assigned to you, do not forget to travel as much as your situation allows. Yes, it costs some money, but the dollars spent will buy you some unforgettable sights and experiences. Plan ahead and make arrangements with the children's teachers if you are unable to travel during school vacation. Most of all, prepare your trips well and don't take any unnecessary health and safety risks. Immunizations must not be overlooked as mentioned earlier. Shortcuts in this department will haunt you. You might get off easy and spend a few uncomfortable days strapped to the toilet seat, or you could be plagued for the rest of your life by something as obnoxious as hepatitis.

Before you travel, it is also a good idea to check with the U.S. State Department on safety guidelines for U.S citizens. Expats tend to forget that they are still citizens of the country whose passport they carry. After so much time, well, it is easy to become a bit relaxed with regard to these minor details. Beware! Political situations keep changing and need to be evaluated. Take precautions, but do try to explore the area around you! Chances are that once you are back home you will never have the same opportunity as you do while you are on site. Never in my life would I have thought of visiting all sorts of tropical paradises: Tahiti, Fiji, Vanuatu. No expats have ever said that they wished they had written more and better memos. Most regret not having seen enough of the area where they spent so much time. They also bemoan the fact that they did not learn more about the culture that they were so intimately associated with.

My friend Sally spent years becoming proficient at being miserable. Her husband was good company. He felt that going anywhere at all was a waste. Too expensive! Who wants to pay that much for an experience and a memory or two? But these are the memories that warm the heart. You'll never forget the yellow fever shots, but neither will you forget the adventure tied to them. As Rosalind Russell said in the movie *Auntie Mame*: "Life is a banquet and most poor bastards are starving to death." Don't become one of those. There is so much excitement that you can share with your partner and with your children: Asian temples, the camera safari in Kenya, the train trip in Switzerland, fly-fishing in Scotland, the opera in Sydney! Go ahead, grasp at the chance while you can.

There are so many creative ways of how you can immerse yourself into the expat experience. Sometimes one just has to get the braces off one's brain in order to see all the opportunities. In the end, it is up to you to fashion your own adventure. Your efforts and your attitude will determine whether your stay will be a success or a disappointment.

Now that you got a life, you pick up speed once again. You

stand tall and head home. Well done! You have successfully negotiated the emotional waves all the way to the shores of the new land.

HUMOR BREAK
THE TROPICAL PARADISE

This is Fantasy Island, I tell you the truth.
The hostess just spoiled us with orchids and juice.
The tour leader waves and up pulls the bus.
He raises his flags and signals for us.
We cruise the main drag. The palms gently sway.
"So where are the locals?"—"They're not on our way."
We zoom right along. It is all a blur.
"Club Med is in town, look over there, Sir.
The elite comes to us, it's no great surprise,
to enjoy themselves right here in paradise.
Sit back and relax. Get used to the notion
that we serve no beer, only love potion.
At five bucks a glass, you got a good price.
And now how about some papaya and rice?
Over here lady, come lounge in the sun.
don't let some cellulite spoil all of the fun."

We dance to the drums on the beach every night.
But, ouch, my poor skin feels ever so tight.
I'm burned to a crisp which could be foreseen.
Why did I neglect to slap on my "fifteen "?
They keep us so busy. We play every sport.
But what do you do when you leave the resort?
Go to the market. They say it's great fun.
But don't drink the water. It will make you run.
Buy T-shirts and trinkets all made in Hong Kong.
It's now or it's never, so shop right along

Now all this exertion put us to the test.
I want to go home for some well-deserved rest.
Once more mango for breakfast, one more sunrise
this is our last day in the tropical paradise.

A Word about Self-Esteem

As we have seen earlier, a lack of challenge and goals can become deadly enemies of expat spouses who are slow in getting a life for themselves. Naturally, at the start of an expat assignment, a period of such enormous change, everybody should be allowed to feel a bit displaced and apprehensive. Brief periods of self-pity and boredom can even be tolerated. However, intense feelings of worthlessness, of rejection or of not being appreciated that seem to last for ever and that interfere with one's normal everyday functioning could be symptoms of a much deeper problem: the plunging of one's notion of "self" which for many ends up in depression.

An insidious downspiraling of one's self-esteem and self-worth is not an uncommon complaint among expat spouses. In our group those who used to have a steady career were especially affected. We felt as though half of our selves had been excised. A lot of time was spent discussing how we had no mission, no focus and no authority. We had become nobodies. What ever for?? We mourned the past.

One day Kate called the appliance rental place and put in an order for a clothes dryer. The guy at the other end politely took the information. Then he told her that he would have to call her husband at the office so that the deal could be finalized and authorized. The woman was beside herself. She used to run a department with 20 people back home, and now she could not even order a clothes dryer! We were all shocked and outraged. How sensitive we all had become! The fact that the order needed to be processed through the company was simply a business detail. The husband had the job, the working permit and the expense account.

Not having our own paychecks anymore proved to be most aggravating. One lady stated that losing her own income was like having the rug pulled out from under her feet. We used to be worth something. Somebody paid us for our time, our efforts, our expertise! Now we were just dependents. If I learned one thing on expat duty, it is that self-worth is not measured in dollar amounts.

Of course, money stands for control and independence, but don't let the money issue interfere with your happiness as an expat. If not having your very own wages really bothers you, make arrangements so that you never have to ask for money. Most importantly, talk about your feelings with your partner. But as life goes on, you will see that this stumbling block also decreases in size. You find out pretty soon that with all of the impending tasks and responsibilities, you earn every penny that comes your way and then some. You will earn your keep. No worries!

When we went home on our first leave, I visited a few big book stores in an attempt to locate material that would shed some light on my plight. But what exactly was my problem? After all, I considered myself a happy, active person. I did not enjoy being depressed and morose. I knew sort of instinctively that the answer would lie within me rather than outside or around me. It is amazing how easy the self-diagnosis became once I stood in front of the self-help shelves. Topics dealing with personal crisis management and self-esteem issues made a lot of sense. I returned overseas well stocked in reading supplies.

I came to realize that my "self "needed a major overhaul. As a matter of fact I had to find it first. Problems with self-worth and self-esteem had plagued me for some time. I focused too much for too long on external rewards and on feedback from others to keep me going and to validate me: grades in school, success and approval at work, knowledge, praise from family and friends. My work defined who I was. I had become what I did! What a shocker! I was never really aware of that.

No wonder that my world crumbled as the wobbly stilts that held me up collapsed. Our move abroad and the loss of my job and support system threw me out of my rut and confronted me with anxieties and insecurities that I had suppressed all of my life. Going on expatriate duty was not the cause of my predicament. It was merely the catalyst that changed the everyday rules and routines enough for the deficiencies within me to reveal themselves. External circumstances got the blame for problems stemming from internal inadequacies. And I was not the only one to whom this happened.

Like myself, many others had also lived for too long with the illusion of being self-assured and self-confident. Many others also measured their self-esteem and self-worth by irrelevant parameters. Overseas duty also shook their 'pseudo-self-esteem,' as Nathaniel Branden the self-esteem guru calls it, in its weak foundation.

You might say: "Sure, sooner or later these ghosts would have come to haunt you anyway." This is perfectly true. But if it happens while you are displaced, on foreign territory, far away from your support system and possible sources of help, the upset packs a double punch at a time when you really do not need the extra stress and turmoil.

As you see, there is literally more to expat duty than what meets the eye. Here are some book suggestions just in case that you come down with a bruised 'core' that needs some emergency care while in a foreign land.

Nathaniel Branden offers a wide variety of topics on the subject of self-esteem. My favorite was "The Power of Self-

Esteem." The information is easy to read, easy to understand and was of great comfort to me. Dazzling professional expressions and big words are not used.

I also liked Dr. Wayne W. Dyer's "Your Erroneous Zones." He has a rather no-nonsense, amusing way of looking at life which gave me a few good laughs. I connected immediately with his candid observations on approval-seeking behaviors. Besides gaining a lot of insight, I also learned that somewhere in my travels I had misplaced a most important survival tool, namely my sense of humor!

Dealing with the Local Population

Don't be too shocked if you find that there are places in this world where people are not as politically and technically correct as you think they should be. As an expat your limits of patience and tolerance might be tested at times. But you are well prepared, and you stay cool under pressure!

Under normal circumstances, one of the big responsibilities of the expat spouse is to handle the local population tactfully. Spouses are out-and-about more than the working partners are. The partners deal with the business end of the expat experience. Spouses deal more with the everyday-life, human aspects. They truly are ambassadors for their country and their company.

Unless you live in semi seclusion in some foreigners' compound, getting acquainted with local residents will add some zest to your days. It gets you out of the cycle of being solely dependent on other expats for company. As a spouse with local connections you also turn into a priceless asset for your partner and for the business that you both represent. In return, the local people meet some of the other expats through you. The gain from all this exposure is mutual. Here we got an example of intercultural exchange at its best.

Making local connections is not only one of the delights of overseas duty, but it is ultimately tied to the success of the assignment. Actually, the faster you meet people from the area, the faster you feel a part of the whole experience. Don't be offended though if you are not greeted immediately with open arms. Luckily you did your homework, and you know that not everybody considers a slap on the back and an invitation to a barbecue as a proper way to get cozy. There simply are societies where people are more formal and a bit cooler towards strangers.

If communication is not your talent, you might want to improve yourself before you leave. Getting prepared will tame some of the anxiety that unfamiliar social situations might bring about. Read a few books on how to chat more effectively and thoughtfully. Larry King, the champion talkmeister, gives some helpful hints in his book:" How to Talk to Anyone, Anytime, Anywhere." It is easy to read, entertaining and, most of all, common sense. Libraries and book stores offer a tremendous amount of choices in the self-help sections. Go ahead, try it!

You might let your hosts take the first step to offer their assistance or to extend an invitation to meet for lunch or tea. Show honest interest in the local history and customs. Generally people are proud of their country and of their heritage. Out of this grows a natural desire to show strangers around and to teach them about their new home. There is nobody like the locals to give tips on proper behavior, where to eat out, what foods to try, what sights to see. At times it is more important to listen and to learn than it is to talk up a storm.

Whenever you deal with the local population remember to always be respectful and humble. It is important not to ridicule local customs or to make negative comments regarding the establishment in general. Coming from a western country, the temptation is great to lecture others on old favorites such as civil rights, animal rights, freedom of speech or across-the-board equality for both humans and beasts. We have an opinion and we state it regardless of the hurt feelings or of the controversy that it might generate in our hosts.

Aren't you fortunate once more that you did your homework ahead of time? You found out about the status of both civil and human rights in your country. You have decided that you can cope with the situation in spite of your own convictions and beliefs. You have decided that you will teach by example: you revere nature, and you treat all people with kindness and respect.

It has been quite embarrassing to be present when lengthy and haughty tirades delivered by uncool expats infuriated multicultural audiences. Criticism and displays of animosity never further the cause of peace and of business. Words are the weapons that hurt the soul. Wounded souls hardly ever heal. Always remember that you are a guest. You are in your host country to do a job! You are not a U.N. envoy, not a missionary, not a politician. You are there to earn a living. Never forget the purpose of your stay.

At least until you know your hosts quite well, topics dealing with religion, sex and politics are best avoided since there is almost a built-in guarantee that you'll offend somebody in a major way. Usually such subjects are not icebreakers. Instead they tend to be icemakers. Isn't that common sense? Doesn't everybody know that? Yet, if you listen to the conversations around you, it becomes apparent that common sense rules are often ignored by people when socializing.

Be careful with alcohol! Alcohol loosens tongues and breaks down inhibitions. This is not just an old wives' tale. Some countries have beverages with so much 'proof' that they pose serious threats to a maybe stellar expat career! Yet, often you almost have to drink along with your hosts in order not to upset them. Get prepared and find out beforehand what the drinking customs of your host country are. Ask about this when you attend your cultural training sessions! Is there a diplomatic way of how you can at least moderate your alcohol intake? You represent yourself, your country and your company. Don't get inebriated because you will still be held responsible for your behavior no matter what you register on the breathalyzer! Besides, it's great to remember in the morning what went on the night before.

An American manager on tour to an Asian country torpedoed himself skyward with some remark that he apparently made while 'being social' with his counterpart's wife. According to him, he told her some innocent joke which the hostess either did not understand or found offensive. She mentioned the incident to her husband who became quite annoyed, to say the least. It did not matter that they all had a bit too much to drink. It did not matter that the foreigner was not used to the local brew. In his hosts' minds there was no excuse for his stepping out of bounds. His off-color kidding had the same effect as a bullet going straight for the foot. The home office was not amused.

This story also makes it clear that it is best to be very cautious with jokes. Most of them are not worth repeating anyway. Besides, senses of humor are fickle and vary greatly from culture to culture.

Social situations can become awfully tricky as you hop across cultural barriers. Some people have the tendency to compare everything that comes their way to how it is in their homeland. From the public transport system to kitchen appliances to the fit of locally made underwear, nothing escapes their criticism. Incessant negativity kills the good mood of those in attendance in a hurry. Statements such as 'this would never work in our country,' 'are we ever spoiled at home' or 'at home we do it this way' can freeze an audience instantly. Such comments make the listeners feel inferior and thus put them on the defensive. I have witnessed a few break-downs in communication due to resentment and hurt feelings brought on by similar insensitive remarks.

Now let's look briefly at the other side of the coin. Generally speaking, I found that people overseas were quite interested in the U.S. They all had seen plenty of specials on TV. Those who had not visited here expressed the desire to see the ever fascinating west and so on. This is the easy part. But—as an expat—how would you react if your hosts ever criticized your homeland? High crime rates in the U.S., our messy health care situation, the plight of the homeless and the aged as well as our legal system became frequent topics for discussion. A lady asked me once if I had friends in the U.S. The question rather stunned me. The reasoning was not so far fetched. With everybody suing everyone else, how can there be any trust upon which to build friendships? One guy quasi joked when he commented that Americans don't talk, they sue. At home one might agree with some of these finer points. However, when one is homesick and displaced in a foreign land, one tends to become annoyed after a while. Think about what you would say! How can some of these truths be put into perspective? If you take up the issue, how can you go on the defensive without being abrasive? As an expat you must be ready to deal with these types of situations in a dignified manner.

If you are female, you will come across some chauvinists. At times you might find yourself in situations of obvious discrimination. How do you handle yourself in this case? This is another detail that your cultural training should address so that you can be prepared. I decided that my time as an expat was limited. Since I was not faced with discrimination at the workplace, the incidents were never major. As a spouse I felt that it was not worth the aggravation to lecture or to confront an offender. I let it go and trusted that karma would eventually even the score. Pick your battles.

There are locations where it becomes quite tedious to meet the local people because they are physically separated from the foreigners. Expats have their own quarters, complete with hospitals, grocery stores and schools, similar to a military base. Some countries are not all too excited about their people mixing with and being influenced by strangers. This does not mean that the local population is totally unreachable. Usually the only time you'll meet is at official business functions. But even at work, contact between the natives and the foreigners might be kept to a cool, professional minimum.

Attention ladies!

In a segregated society wives are usually not invited to social events. If they are, they might be separated from the men. Women run the risk of dual isolation, because they are foreigners and because they are women. Call it chauvinism, racism or whatever label you want to stick on such practices. The bottom line is that some cultures do not believe that women are equal to men. Luckily, you have done your homework! You have researched all the details with regard to the social situation of women. You have decided that you will bundle-up even in blistering heat. The morals police will not phase you. You know that you will not be bothered by the fact that you cannot go out by yourself. You will not mind that you are not allowed to drive. You accept that—outside of the confines of your living quarters at least—your husband is your master.

If you accept such an assignment you must be convinced that you can handle the situation! Beware! There is a big difference between learning something from a book or in a course and actually living it! The limitations on personal freedom can greatly curtail the enjoyment that female spouses get out of such overseas stays. Then again, if they have the chance to chat with some local women, it might change their whole outlook on life. It could be horizon-expanding-time !

Incidentally, men often find the assignments in the more mystical, male-oriented places quite fascinating. Maybe the whole setup caters to their dominator mentality, but sometimes impressive money incentives also get them to sign up again and again. Of course, males have more rights in such societies than females do. Therefore they are less affected by the isolation that typically plagues the ladies. If you consider such an assignment, come to an understanding about the exact length of the proposed stay. Then again, I know one spouse who agreed to two years but who has just started her sixth. Her husband does not want to leave for all sorts of reasons.

Most women agree though that they had some unforgettable experiences. Stints in Saudi Arabia have been described as magical, surreal, mirage-like but difficult and cumbersome because of the imposed restrictions. "Enjoy, but keep it short," is probably the most honest suggestion that I heard.

Of course, you are a polite, caring and diplomatic person. Of course, you respect people of all colors, sizes and shapes. So why even talk about these rules that are so elementary, so basic? Because it is quite easy to fall out of step when one feels under pressure, lonesome, annoyed, displaced and maybe disappointed with one's assignment. A disastrous faux pas on the social scene, however, might spell disaster in the business arena. Upsetting the hosts is another reason why an expat career can come to an abrupt end.

Always observe the rules of common courtesy! This is a sound philosophy in life, especially in expat life. Treat other people the way you would like to be treated. That way you avoid stepping on toes and, most of all, you will not embarrass yourself.

Friends Overseas

While abroad, you will get close to some of the other expats and hopefully also to some of the local people. I can tell you from experience though that, while trying to forge new friendships, you should not forget about those friends whom you left behind at home.

Building relationships takes time. Yet time is a luxury that expats often do not have enough of. Think of expatriates as modern-day gypsies. They camp out for so long, then they douse the glowing ashes and move on. You will leave. You know it. Everybody knows it. Expect people to be very protective of their personal lives since the expatriate situation by its very nature puts a time limit on any relationship. Nobody wants to get too attached then end up hurt. Instinctively, we all protect our inner core. A gentleman once stated that expat friendships are a lot like military friendships: one minute you all walk to the same beat, but when the music stops, folks scatter and go their own way.

Sue was on her first overseas assignment with her husband. She became very distressed when Barb, one of the other expat ladies whom she particularly liked, was sent to another location. Worse yet, Sue really never heard from Barb anymore. But they were buddies, pioneers, the first two families on site! Sue was very upset. As she became a bit more experienced and hard-nosed, Sue realized that expat relationships are wonderful . . . while they last.

I would guess that most expat contacts do not progress far past the stage of comfortable companion. This is not only true for relationships between expats themselves but also for those between expats and locals. Many of us agree that the bonds formed during our years in exile were quite fragile. We met for lunch. We went to a movie now and then. We organized a barbecue on special occasions. Yes, we all were 'friends.' But in retrospect, I must admit that I knew very little about the personal lives of any of these people and that they probably knew even less about me.

The closeness of an expatriate community depends a lot on the location of the assignment. It would make sense that, the greater the language barrier, the more numerous the cultural road blocks, the more isolated the site, the tighter the bonds between the expats should be. As a rule expats stick together while on assignment. Even people who under normal circumstances would probably not see eye-to-eye share a common bond. It is the feeling of being in the same boat that draws expatriate communities together. I never had a problem getting a ride if I needed one, or finding somebody to chat with when I felt a bit lonely.

Before we shipped out I was told various times: "Don't worry! You might be separated from your own family for a while, but you'll find a new family in those with whom you share the adventure."

I once asked a lady who lived in Singapore with her husband if she found that there was some truth to other expats becoming one's family. She said that even though their group was well organized, her impression was that the ties between the individuals tended to be quite loose. She reported that her fellow expats made efforts to have regularly scheduled parties. They had formed a choir and published their own little newspaper to keep each other informed of happenings. In spite of all those activities, she conceded that there was hardly any opportunity to develop cozy family type relationships due to the revolving-door syndrome. "By the time you get to know people a bit, they leave," she added. "After a while, you get tired of continuously starting all over again."

Especially in the beginning of the adventure, new expats do not miss a chance to attend every picnic and coffee klatsch that they can find. The spouses are eager to meet other spouses. The kids get introduced to one another. Now and then whole families will set out for drives in search of adventure and exciting vistas. At lunches and at parties the novelty of the experience keeps the conversation going. To outsiders such expat groups look like one big, happy family! People compare notes, discuss their experiences and share their feelings—up to a certain point.

Real problems faced by individuals, such as personal matters or family crises, are usually not discussed. Expats often report that they never talked to anyone about those issues that bothered them the most, that caused them sadness and maybe even sorrow and pain. The question that keeps surfacing is how much does one want business associates or business rivals to know about the more intimate details of one's life? Business undertones usually manage to keep up a certain barrier when it comes to friendships and family ties among expats. In the end, 'expat families' will never replace your mom or dad, uncle Henry or aunt Sue.

Remember that even in the homeland you do not bare your soul to just anybody. But there you have different options. You have a variety of people to whom you can talk, with whom you can consult, in whom you can confide. Overseas your options are naturally more limited. This is yet another reason why it is so important to have a solid relationship with your partner. You are each other's support and family. You must be able to discuss all of those problems that you cannot and maybe should not share with outsiders. With this much said, you see already why it is pretty important to keep in touch on a regular basis with relatives and friends back home.

As time passes, the expat network that at first seemed ever

so tight will relax. The number of spouse meetings decreases. There are more people who have conflicts and cannot attend the barbecue. This is quite normal. Folks are settling in their new environment. By and by they meet other people with whom they share interests. They get involved in activities that demand some of their time and that give them satisfaction. The novelty of the big move wears off.

Contacts with very weak ties are the specialty of the professional expats. These are the folks who accept consecutive out-of-country assignments and who do not take root easily. In fact, with every tour of duty they become more aloof. They are interesting, challenging and maybe amusing, but they have no problem turning their backs on those whom they 'befriended.' They are simply too independent in order to attach themselves to anyone. I met some of these site-hoppers, and I must admit that talking to them was a fascinating and often uplifting experience. They had a lot of tales to tell—especially Jack—and I learned quite a bit by just listening.

Maybe the bonds of expat friendships and of extended family ties will last forever. Good for you! I certainly know some people who found their closest friends while on foreign assignment. Sandra told me that the most precious friends in her life are still those that she made among the locals while on overseas duty with her husband. She keeps in regular contact by writing, E-mailing and calling, and her friends reciprocate. Why do I feel a whopping reunion coming on one of those days?

If it happens that one finds soul mates either among the other expats or among the local people, it is great. Who would ever have trouble dealing with such success and good fortune? The problem arises when we are in Sue's situation, when we feel neglected by people to whom we felt closer than we actually were.

Don't let fears of being left behind make you miss out on meeting people from all walks of life, one of the most rewarding and enriching aspects of the whole expat experience. Enjoy your time overseas. Get to know as many people from as many different backgrounds as you can. Learn and observe! This is your chance. The time will come all too soon when you must turn your back and fly off into the sunset.

With these thoughts in mind, do not forget about your friends that you left behind in the homeland. Don't take them for granted. You know how precious real friendships are. They need to be maintained and cared for like a piece of art. Write, E-mail, call! By the time you return home for good, life will have changed and the familiar face of a good friend will be a welcome sight.

HUMOR BREAK
CHRISTMAS OVERSEAS

So this is Christmas, the end of the year!
But why can't I muster up any good cheer?
There is no ice, no cold and no snow.
For here Down Under it is summer you know.

It's blistering and swampy, and I cannot shop.
I guess this year I shall sweat till I drop.
Where are my friend Cathy, my sis and aunt Sue?
I am quite homesick. Don't know what to do.

The tinsel, the pine tree look terribly fake.
But Santa in shorts! Oh, give me a break!
A 'barbie' with burgers, chicken and prawn
replaces the turkey, the gravy, the corn.

It's too hot to cook. There's no pie as a treat,
so I try some Pavlova and fruit as a sweet.

As midnight draws near the cicadas all hush.
Kangaroos pull the sleigh up through the brush.

Santa drops presents off right at the door
since we have no chimneys for him to aim for.
I catch myself dreaming as the moon rises high
I feel that I had Christmas right smack in July.

Holidays Abroad

From a sentimental point of view, holidays abroad are one of the toughest parts of the adventure. You spend these special events with those who have joined you in your voluntary exile.

The first Thanksgiving overseas was weird. Turkey is not a national food in all countries. One has to understand this in order to deal with the sad excuses that impersonate the ever popular gobbler. For us the word 'Butterball' was stricken from the vocabulary. Our bird resembled a skinny, stringy, overgrown duck. Whatever we had on our first Thanksgiving was probably a lot closer to what the Pilgrims ate since Jennie-O was not in business yet in those days.

But what is wrong with having goose or capon at Thanksgiving ? It does not taste the same, and it is against tradition! You guessed it. Then again, expatriates find out quickly that a lot of things are not the same, taste the same, look the same or smell the same as they do at home. You can cope with these facts most of the time. For holidays, however, you demand your comfort food. Aunt Mary has to send an old shoe box packed with canned sweet potatoes and cranberries or else! But can we not be thankful while eating stir fry, curry or tabouli? Will we let the absence of gravy spoil the most American of all holidays? Of course not! Expats improvise!

There are so many personal memories attached to holidays. Your family might be one of those with all sorts of special holiday traditions !

You probably never appreciated aunt Roberta's Christmas accordion concert or uncle Nick's New Year's Limburger cheese party! How about mother! She could not wait to get everybody together for the holidays. Then she felt promptly overwhelmed. Remember how there was always something wrong with the turkey? Mom would cuss under her breath in the kitchen because it stuck to the pan, because there was not enough juice for gravy, because it was too dry, too small, too big ! Same story every time! Now you miss it all !

Learning to appreciate what you left behind is yet another benefit derived from expat life. Lessons in gratitude are learned very quickly.

Many expats, especially if children are involved, try to make their trip to the homeland around Christmas. What about those who stay behind? Dave, the senior member of our group, once suggested at a holiday gathering that we should assume the role of being one another's family. "Think of me as your dad," he said. It was one of those times when the thought of an extended expat family proved to be comforting.

Holidays are the perfect time to follow E.T.'s example and to phone home! A call from Biloela, Australia, might just get a rise out of your folks! It does feel good now and then to hear familiar voices. This human connection beats E-mail and the computer super-highway hands-down. Who needs Cyberspace? Give me uncle Buck live, please! The telephone is probably the most appreciated and comforting piece of modern equipment that an expat can have.

Sure, it is great to hear a loved one's voice! But doesn't the cost of the calls sour the holiday spirit? With the explosion of international business, many communication companies cash in on lonesome expats by offering reduced overseas telephone rates. One of our more money conscious colleagues came up with a global access company called "TELE-GROUP" which is located in Fairfield, Iowa. Their substantially lower rates made all the difference in the world to me. I could call my sister in Europe and keep in touch with some people back home. Even with the advantageous rates, our phone bills were still higher than other families' mortgage payments, but at least we did not go bankrupt. Check on budget long distance phone companies in your assigned location. It is well worth the effort.

Holidays are unique because they open little windows that let us peek at a nation's history and cultural heritage. Invite a few of your local friends and neighbors to celebrate some of your holidays with you. Chances are extremely high that your offer will not be turned down. Humans are curious by nature and want to learn.

Depending on where you are located and on how well you know your prospective guests, Thanksgiving might be ideal. All cultures can relate to the thought of giving thanks. Some interesting discussions will surely be sparked. What kind of implications did the Pilgrims' celebration have for the native people? It was certainly interesting to hear different points of view!

If you are lucky enough and find at least some of the necessary ingredients, fix a traditional dinner as best you can. In our area, pumpkin pie certainly was the star attraction. Locally pumpkin soup is a popular dish. People also bake pumpkin as we do squash, but the thought of 'pie' raised a few eyebrows initially. Cranberries are always a novelty. Since they are hard to find overseas, pack a couple of cans before you leave. People want to know where they grow, how they are harvested and what they look and taste like before they are cooked or canned.

Holidays offer a great opportunity to open some dialogue

with local people. This might be your chance to ask a few questions of your own regarding some of the festivities of your host country. Who knows? Maybe you'll get yourself an invitation to join the celebrations on Anzac Day, May Day, Kartini Day. If you do, read up and give it a try.

Keep in Touch with Home

Once you are on overseas assignment, why do you feel like going home for a visit? Family and friends are the obvious drawing cards, of course. But there is another reason: it is extremely important to show up periodically at our old place of work. It is simply not a good idea to drop totally out of sight and out of mind with the home office. Never let them forget who you are, where you are and how to spell your name. This is not only vital for the working partner, but also for the spouse. It is wise to keep the communication channels open on both sides.

Spouses! Think of the future. One of those days your tour will come to a close. Therefore, it is bad practice to let professional ties disintegrate or to miss the chance of making new contacts on the home front. Don't be like Diane. She became somewhat despondent over the fact that her employer could not guarantee her a position upon her return. She even let her professional license lapse!! Unbelievable! Even if you do not keep in touch with your previous employer or colleagues, never ever let a professional license expire! Pay your dues, do the continuing education, do whatever it takes to stay current and licensed in your field of practice.

A spouse might have quit his or her job when going on expat duty, but this does not mean that he or she has given up all plans for a future career. The working partner does not want to run the risk either of simply being forgotten somewhere in the snowfields of Siberia. This is why it is so important to visit and to phone the home base on a regular basis. Remind them of your presence!

After years of absence Rick was very discouraged that the company did not have a major new assignment waiting for him when he returned home. He was amazed when he saw who sat at his old desk. He was somewhat puzzled when he found out who had been promoted in his absence. So much had happened while he was gone! Seriously bitten by the travel bug, Rick had never bothered to come back to the homeland on some of his vacations. He never called the home office unless it was strictly business. He had never met the new department head, and he had not seen his colleagues in ages. Big mistake!

The world is ruled by those who show up and by those who happen to stand around when the boss needs a 'body' to fill a vacancy or to cater to an immediate business need. "Smithers would be great in this capacity," they might say, "but unfortunately he is in Java right now having a good time. Looks like he wants to stay on. He never calls, and he has never informed us of any future plans. So let's promote Williams instead."

Once you are abroad, don't become complacent. Together with your partner review your situation from time to time. If the correct opportunity came up, could you be swayed to consider it? What would such opportunities be? What positions will be vacated back home that might pique your interest at some time in the future? Knowing what you know now, would you take on a second expatriate assignment? What new ventures is the company going into? What new sites have been added lately to the list? It is obvious that it will be very hard to make any future plans unless you keep your finger on the pulse of the happenings in the main office.

Whenever we went home for a visit, I dropped in at my old job for a chat with friends, lunch in the cafeteria and a talk with my former boss. It was very important to me to keep in touch with my own contacts. Not only did I catch up on some gossip, but I also learned what was new in my field of practice. Stepping back into my own world also proved to be somewhat of a cleansing and healing experience for me. It gave me back the feeling of professional belonging that I craved so much at times.

My husband always made sure that he spent time at the home office whenever we went back to the U.S. This gave him an insight into new developments, and it opened the door for a lunch or a dinner with his colleagues. The revelations that popped out on such occasions were well worth the effort and every minute spent. Sometimes one personal appearance beats a hundred E-mail messages.

The fact that you are far away from home right now does not mean that it will always be that way. Keep up with company politics and gossip! When the topic of 'repatriation' comes up, you will be glad that you did.

V

How Do I Successfully Return from Assignment?

Repatriation— Those Waves Again!

How time flies! You have finally tackled the daily routines in your host country, and now the moment has already come to think of going back home. Time to pack, to call the movers, to say goodbye to your new friends and acquaintances! Repatriation is the reverse of expatriation. It involves a lot of work and planning and even some sadness. I spent a good portion of my last year preparing myself emotionally and professionally for the return to the old homestead. I expected some reverse culture shock and I was not wrong. People who had repatriated before us told me that it took close to a year for them to feel at home again in the city and in the house that they had left years earlier. It would make sense that the longer one has been away, the more traumatic repatriation will be.

As you get ready to leave your post, don't be surprised that you have to ride the whole emotional wave cycle all the way back to the homeland. As it was in the beginning of the adventure so it will be in the end. You will have up and down swings until you finally settle into a predictable daily routine. Can you sense some treacherous emotional waves lapping at your feet? Take the surfboard out of storage and hang on! Just in case that you misplaced your nautical chart, the re-patriation waves are shown in Figure #3 on the next page.

The thought of going back to your own place will certainly elicit some feelings of elation. It will be good to go home! You are up. But then again, you feel a bit depressed about leaving your host country, the sights, the friends and maybe even the life that has become second nature to you. You know your host country better by now then you know your home country. All of the work and turmoil surrounding the impending move bear down on you once again. You begin to fade. But you know the feeling. After the ups and downs you head for the doldrums which precede your move home.

You step off the plane. Great to be home! You're on the re-verse globe-trotter high. You are ready to rediscover what you left behind a while ago. You are excited. But what happened? 'Home' is different. The coziness factor might not be as high as you thought it should be. Again the initial surges of elation are dampened by a weird sensation of being displaced on your own turf. You might feel more like a new-comer than an old familiar fixture. This too shall pass! After all, you are just starting yet another new phase of your life, and beginnings are rarely without glitches. Give yourself some time to let your feet touch the ground. Gradually you'll reshape your life. Once more you complete your surf ride successfully by defining your new niche in your old home.

I must add that even though we had visited on a regular basis, I was actually amazed that the thought of moving home scared me somewhat. My period of being elated was very brief. For others it lasted for months. I had just become

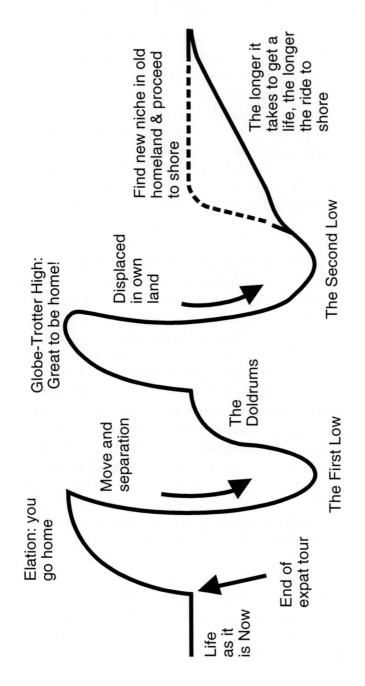

The Emotional Waves
Figure #3

really comfortable in our home abroad. I had made some friends, and I had gained acceptance in the community. Most of all, I had gotten somewhat used to the climate. Telling me to pack up once again was like asking me to abandon all those bridges that I had so tediously built over the last few years. I thought: "Here today, gone tomorrow! No wonder many people do not care to get too close to expats."

Why did I feel apprehensive about moving back? After all, "home is where they love ya, baby!" I had not lived in my house, city and neighborhood for years. I was not used to noise and to high traffic levels anymore. Time to relearn how to drive on the right-hand side of the road! All those anxieties! How could they be tamed? So much had changed! I was pushing 50. I had no job! My masseuse had closed up shop! The house needed some major TLC and so did I.

Some companies have formal programs designed to help expats with the process of returning home. In the months before the actual move, a repatriation trip might be offered in order to allow you to make all the necessary arrangements for a smooth transition to the homeland. Don't be too optimistic though! You might be offered some help with the physical move, but chances are that there will not be a great deal of emotional support. Why think of the psychological trauma that repatriates can go through? Isn't going home easy?

I can tell you from personal experience that I was much better prepared for leaving on assignment than I was for returning home. Providing adequate assistance to repatriating workers is a much neglected area in international business. So, help yourself and God and the company will help you!

As your assignment draws to a close, take out your checklists and prepare to do everything all over that you did when you moved to your expatriate site:

- Call the home office and make sure that the responsible people are indeed aware of your imminent repatriation. It would be logical to assume that they should know already but many employers have hundreds of expats all over the world at any given time. Now and then it is hard to keep track of every move of every individual.
- If you sold your home before you left, you might want to get in touch with a real estate agent and sort out your preferences for a new house or apartment.
- Call the storage company and let them know when you will need your stored goods delivered. The human resource department might make some of these arrangements for you, but I felt better doing it myself. That way I knew that things were taken care of.
- Do you know where the children will go to school after your return? Got any thoughts on new cars?
- If you, the spouse, plan to go back to work upon your return put out feelers for a new job ahead of time. Make contact with some of your old partners and bosses and see what the market is like. Aren't you glad that you kept in touch with the home base while you were abroad?
- If you kept your house, the time has come to notify the property manager of your return. The renters must be given notice. You might consider having the manager arrange for a professional cleaning before you move back in. If there are any repairs or painting to be done, now could be a good time to do this. The repatriation allowance that your company hopefully provides is meant to take care of at least some of these expenses.
- Before you leave your overseas location, don't forget to secure transcripts from your children's schools. Also get a copy of any health records if you have received medical care abroad.
- Working partners should ask for a final performance

evaluation from their boss. If you, the spouse, have worked or volunteered in any way also get a letter documenting your efforts.

- Find out from your tax specialist or financial advisor what special documents you should secure for your future tax statements. Will you need bank documents related to the liquidation of your overseas accounts? Do you need any statements from the local tax office or from the immigration department?

Some human resource departments meet with the returning expats in what might be called a debriefing session. They ask for feedback, what was good and bad about the experience, what assistance is needed to help others relocate without major drama.

Expect Some Changes — Reverse Culture Shock

It is quite normal for expatriates to idealize their homeland once they are far away from it. They dream of how things are better, kinder, gentler and more efficient back there. It is natural to forget about the negative and to only remember the positive while they are stranded in some remote land. The mere thought of 'home' gives them that warm, fuzzy feeling. So, as returning expats they might expect to be welcomed back with the city band serenading them as they step off the plane. Forget it!

For spouses who have lived a life of luxury while they were abroad, repatriation can be tough. From having a driver and servants they are suddenly faced once again with the reality of doing their daily chores themselves. This has been described as one big letdown!

Repatriation can also be especially traumatic for those expats who have neglected to go on home leave now and then. They discover that home suddenly feels like a foreign land.

They find that the world has not stood still waiting for their return. The changes that took place in their absence often come as a major shock and disappointment. Why? Because they did not keep in touch with their home base while on assignment, and because they had unreasonable expectations of what their homecoming would be like.

There is no doubt that you, the spouse, will have plenty of problems and questions of your own upon repatriation. However, try not to be too terribly busy within the first weeks or even months after your return. Your family will need you once more as a reliable support system and emotion manager.

When moving back home, expect some changes!

• The neighborhood has changed.

Some neighbors may have moved away. Favorite stores might have closed. New houses have probably mushroomed. Maybe the local deli had to make way for yet another parking lot.

• Your friends have changed.

Life actually went on during your absence. Your old friends might have had their share of change in their own lives through events that you are not part of unless you kept in touch. After such a long time away, it is almost impossible to pick up friendships where you left off.

Returning expats might be surprised by the inability of their friends to relate to the feelings of anxiety and ambiguity that they experience upon their return from assignment. The friends might have a so-what attitude not because they are mean or jealous, but because they do not understand the emotional waves that often accompany repatriation. In their minds you were pretty lucky to have been given the opportunity to live abroad. So what's the problem? Should this happen to you, don't take it out on your friends. Instead, call your home office or relocation consultants and ask for the names of other repatriated expats in your area. You need to share your experiences and your feelings with somebody who has firsthand knowledge of what you are going through. Besides, it will be good to have some contacts among fellow ex-expats. Get together now and then for a lunch or a picnic. Share some laughs while reminiscing about those wild adventures abroad that will be part of your life forever.

• The city has changed.

New roads and bridges have been built. Suburbs have been added. A park was sacrificed for a shopping mall. Traffic levels have increased. Maybe the crime rate has taken a turn for the worse.

• Your house has changed.

The belongings that you stored a while back also have taken on a different look. Yes, that dingy, dusty, drab stuff is your furniture!

• Job markets have changed.

Career opportunities for you, the spouse, might prove to be elusive. You have been out of the limelight for some time. Your employer might have hit some hard times and fire instead of hire.

The hospital where I used to work for umpteen years closed during our absence. However, this all came as no surprise to me since I had kept in steady contact with the folks back home. I was sad but not too terribly upset since I had grown beyond the confines of my on-line pharmacy job anyway. While we were still overseas I began to completely rethink my life and thus faced a totally new beginning upon my return.

• Dynamics in the home office have changed.

This could be one of the harshest truths faced by the working partners. It can be startling to discover who has been promoted and who has been demoted in their absence. Those who have not kept up with company politics might be in for some major surprises.

The fact that returning expats often do not feel quite welcome in the old work place can make for an uneasy transition. Maybe they sense a certain jealousy among those who stayed behind and also among the new hires. They might not get much assistance from anybody after their lengthy absence. The unasked question among those in the office is whether returning expats will try to pull rank or throw their weight around and show everybody how things are handled in the international arena.

Returning expats might also feel unappreciated by their employers. Surveys have shown that roughly 25% of repatriated workers leave their companies within the first 3 years of returning home. Career stalemates and sheer frustration are often the reasons for jumping ship.

Expatriate life inevitably changes candidates. Being away from the control of the boss at home gave them responsibilities, maybe even power, and a freedom that they now miss. They have learned different ways of doing business. They think globally now and feel that they do not fit any longer into the old mold. Of course, there is something exotic and exciting about duty abroad. It is hard to come back from the Pacific Rim to the office on the Nth floor in a downtown office block.

Again, never expect an employer to just 'take care of you.' Rather than sitting around feeling neglected what can your partner, the returning expat, offer to the company? Encourage him or her to sit down and to make a list of items to share with the bosses.

In the course of his or her assignment what did your partner learn that will add value to the company? What can you, the spouse, contribute?

What are the positive aspects that can be built upon and

encouraged? Maybe the home office called overseas with weekly updates on office developments! Wonderful!

What are the negative points that need to be worked on? Are there policies that are incompatible with the host country's culture? How can they be changed? Was there undue frustration on-site because the home office never answered phone calls or E-mail messages?

Use your knowledge and insight to help employers become more efficient in their overseas business and to help future expats have an easier life.

Especially those expats who never communicated their agenda might find that the company has not made any big plans for their future. There might not even be a personal desk waiting for them. This does not mean that the bosses do not appreciate the ex-expats' talents. They might be surprised by their return and might need some time to determine where they can use such valuable employees best.

When Al returned home from overseas there was no fanfare. He had assumed that everybody knew when he would be back in town. He got stuck into a windowless office and was assigned a known 'loser project.' Even though he felt somewhat rejected, Al kept his cool. He sorted out the mess that he was presented with and kept talking to those in charge. He remembered that he had not been given any career guarantees right from the start. Besides, he had never made his plans known to his department head. He recognized that the delay in action was a bit his fault too. It took a while to find Al's personal niche, but in the end he was made financial officer in charge of the company's most vital overseas contracts.

With this much said, give the boss a chance, and give things some time to settle down. If you do not get a satisfactory assignment, you can always call the headhunter later. As a rule, expats are investments whose acquired knowledge smart companies should not want to waste.

Upon repatriating you find that your friends, the city, your career prospects might all have changed, but most importantly, you discover that

• You All Have Changed.

You are no longer the same people who set out for the big adventure. You are citizens of the world now. It takes some time to get used to that idea. Children often are depressed when they fail to reconnect with old friends. The kids have also been affected by the horizon-expanding experience of their stay abroad. Suddenly their old school as well as their old friends seem pretty provincial to them.

In order to repatriate successfully, keep communicating with your home office, your friends, your business associates and last but not least, your family. Knowing what is happening back home will minimize surprises and help you to manage your expectations. By the time you get off that plane you'll be mentally prepared to accept the fact that you have changed and so has Kansas. As a well-prepared returning expat, you will ride that last wave smoothly to the homeshore, no worries! It will feel good to be back at last on one's own turf again.

VI

Conclusion

When it comes to expatriate assignments the type of job, your family circumstances, the timing of the offer and the proposed location are of course all important. After you analyzed the facts, tested the motives and accepted to relocate, your ATTITUDE, more than anything else, will dictate how much you will get out of the tour. Cling to your surfboard and don't fight the wave! If you see adventure and an opportunity to learn and to grow, then that's what you will find.

At the start, I thought that there could not possibly be any life for me outside of work, outside of my profession. Later on I learned that there is a lot more to one's existence than a standard job. If you can afford it financially, let this be your time for learning. Enjoy the experience. I also found out gradually what my main mission as an expat spouse was: to support my family in a time of tremendous change and to represent the company in the community. By not forcing myself into a fixed schedule, I had a lot more time and patience for doing what was at that point my most important assignment.

I told you in the beginning that I would never surrender the experience of having lived overseas. In conclusion, I want to restate that same point. I am glad that I gave the out-of-country life a try. Had I decided to stay at home in my familiar rut, I would have missed out on an adventure that not only changed my life but that also introduced me to a zillion of 'firsts.'

While I was an expat, I went to my very first horse race, a formal event for which I even invested in a fancy hat.

Formula-1 car racing? I am not a car-nut and never gave this type of thrill a lot of thought. Then we had the good fortune to be taken to the Australian Cup in Melbourne. Marvelous!

How about my friend Josey, the koala? Koalas do not live in Minneapolis. Josey alone made our stay in her country all worthwhile. I miss her a lot!

Would I have had the chance to write a weekly health column for the paper back home? Hardly! Competition and editors with enormous waste baskets tend to turn efforts from unknowns into an exercise in futility. The local people, however, perceived my contribution as a needed community service. So much in life depends on perspective!

Our small town was quite an important spot in Central Queensland. I met all sorts of artists, political party leaders as well as the old and the new Prime Ministers of Australia. I even got to talk to them.

Sweet revenge! I was asked to be a panel judge for a model search and for the bride-of-the-year award contest. Talk about a challenge of a different kind!

Did we have any not-so-good experiences while overseas? Of course, we all got dunked a few times and almost were tossed off the surfboard. Disagreeable surprises loom everywhere. In this regard, however, expat life is a lot like childbirth. After a while you forget about the discomfort, and you remember the pleasant parts of the experience. Maybe I was lucky, but in my case the good by far outweighed the bad. I will always cherish my time abroad.

If you decide to dive into the adventure, do so with an open mind. Life is not perfect no matter where you are. Yet, I guarantee that an expat tour will be a tremendous learning experience, if you give yourself a chance. All of the wisdom and knowledge gained from the venture are assets so valuable that it is impossible to assign them a dollar value. They will be yours forever, totally robbery and inflation proof.

VII

Checklists

TABLE 1
SMITH FAMILY ANNUAL BUDGET

	Existing (stay home)	Expatriate (go)
Income Source		
Salary/Pension Spouse 1	75000	95000
Salary/Pension Spouse 2	40000	0
Investment Income Total	10000	10000
Sub-Total Income	125000	105000
Income Taxes		
Federal Income Tax	21000	15000
State/County/City Income Tax[1]	3000	2500
Social Security/Medicare Tax	8000	5300
Net Income	93000	82200
Expenses		
Mortgage Payment	18000	18000
Property Taxes[2]	3000	3000
House Insurance[2]	800	800
Other Housing expenses	4000	4000
Telephone	1000	4000
Car 1 Loan or Lease Payment	4000	0
Car 2 Loan or Lease Payment	3000	0
Auto Insurance	2000	0
Auto Maintenance/Fuel	2000	0
Groceries and Dining Out[3]	10000	12000
Clothing[3]	5000	5000
Other expenses[4]	12000	12000
Credit Card Payments(on debt)	1000	1000
Total Expenses	65800	59800
Remaining Funds[5]	27200	22400

TABLE 2
ROBINSON FAMILY ANNUAL BUDGET

	Existing (stay home)	Expatriate (go)
Income Source		
Salary/Pension Spouse 1	60000	80000
Salary/Pension Spouse 2	50000	0
Investment Income Total	10000	10000
Sub-Total Income	120000	90000
Income Taxes		
Federal Income Tax	19000	11000
State/County/City Income Tax[1]	2900	2100
Social Security/ Medicare Tax	9200	4600
Net Income	88900	72300
Expenses		
Mortgage Payment	18000	18000
Property Taxes[2]	3000	3000
House Insurance[2]	800	800
Other Housing expenses	4000	4000
Telephone	1000	4000
Car 1 Loan or Lease Payment	4000	0
Car 2 Loan or Lease Payment	3000	0
Auto Insurance	2000	0
Auto Maintenance/ Fuel	2000	0
Groceries and Dining Out[3]	10000	12000
Clothing[3]	5000	5000
Other expenses[4]	12000	12000
Credit Card Payments(on debt)	12000	12000
Total Expenses	76800	70800
Remaining Funds[5]	12100	1500

TABLE 3
YOUR FAMILY ANNUAL BUDGET

	Existing (stay home)	Expatriate (go)
Income Source		
Salary/Pension Spouse 1	_____	_____
Salary/Pension Spouse 2	_____	_____
Investment Income Total	_____	_____
Sub-Total Income	_____	_____
Income Taxes		
Federal Income Tax	_____	_____
State/County/City Income Tax[1]	_____	_____
Social Security/ Medicare Tax	_____	_____
Net Income	_____	_____
Expenses		
Mortgage Payment	_____	_____
Property Taxes[2]	_____	_____
House Insurance[2]	_____	_____
Other Housing expenses	_____	_____
Telephone	_____	_____
Car 1 Loan or Lease Payment	_____	_____
Car 2 Loan or Lease Payment	_____	_____
Auto Insurance	_____	_____
Auto Maintenance/Fuel	_____	_____
Groceries and Dining Out[3]	_____	_____
Clothing[3]	_____	_____
Other expenses[4]	_____	_____
Credit Card Payments (on debt)	_____	_____
Total Expenses	_____	_____
Remaining Funds[5]	_____	_____

NOTES to TABLES 1, 2 and 3

1. Many States require State Income Tax to be paid even while living and working overseas—please check this.

2. Property Taxes and Home Insurance may increase as much as 100% or more, if you do not live in your own house. However, most employers will pay the difference in cost.

3. Dining and Clothing Expenses will generally increase slightly while living overseas, but this can vary a great deal depending upon the circumstances, the family's tastes and the cost of living in the country in which you will be living.

4. Other Expenses include all of the miscellaneous items that we buy. Although the type of items that are purchased may change dramatically while living overseas, generally the level of expenses will remain the same. For example, instead of purchasing items for the home, the family would spend the same dollars on travel and souvenirs. Again, expenses here will vary depending upon the situation.

5. The Smith Family's Remaining Funds will be generally the same whether they go on assignment or not. However the Robinsons' Remaining Funds will be nearly gone if they go on assignment. The Robinsons must evaluate their finances to see how they can reduce expenses in case they plan to become expats. It can be unwise to go on expatriate duty without an adequate financial cushion to handle unexpected expenses.

Decision Making Questionnaire

Even though you are intrigued by the possibility of an expatriate adventure, is it the right move for you and your family?

To help you determine your real feelings I have compiled some checklists of common concerns on four major topics: the job, family matters, the location and quality of life. The purpose here is to make you think about the issues so that you can identify areas that you need to get more information on or that could spell trouble for you and your family. Before you can do any of this work you must have at least some relevant knowledge regarding the job itself and the potential host country. In other words, you must have done your homework!

Instructions

It is best to go through all of the lists first and to just do scoring. After you have scored all items, review the lists and use your scores to identify problem areas. Can you think of possible compromises, solutions or actions that might alleviate the situation? Scrutinize your negative values. As I mentioned before in the book, I found that some of my very strong negatives did not turn out to be major problems. On some items I needed a lot more information. Other dark spots cleared once I talked to people who could give me a firsthand account of life in our host country.

1) Score each item with your first reaction. Try not to dwell on each score. Use a scale of +10 to –10.

+10   you have extremely positive feelings about that item

+7   you have moderately positive feelings about that item

+3   you have slightly positive feelings about that item

0   you are neutral on this item

–3   you have slightly negative feelings about that item

–7   you have moderately negative feelings about that item

–10   you have extremely negative feelings about that item

Use the 0 score sparingly. If you are neutral on too many items, could it be because you are not well enough informed in order to have an opinion?

2) If you do not have enough information, leave the score BLANK. This will provide you with a list of things that you absolutely must collect more facts on.

3) After you have scored all items on all pages, go through the list again and circle all issues which you gave a score of 0 to –10. Naturally it is best for you if you have a lot of strong positives and few weak, if any, negatives. Many strong negatives should make you step back and think hard about expatriate tour.

4) Now review each circled issue and think about possible actions that can be taken in order to alleviate problems. Note these in the comments space. Would more information or education help bring the negatives at least closer to 0 or even into the positive range? Could some compromises be reached?

5) Look at the blank items. How many holes are there in your knowledge? Make a list of questions to ask the employer or the relocation specialists. Before you can tally your final score, you must get resolution on the blank items.

6) Now add the scores on each page and then total all pages. To evaluate your score see the section at the end.

I) *The Job: Based on Your Current Knowledge, How Do You Feel About It?*

Using the previous +10 to −10 scale, score each item with your first reaction. Try not to dwell on each score. Score a 0 if you are neutral on this item. Leave items blank that you cannot answer due to lack of information.

Examples: How do you feel about your potential new boss? Is this a reasonable, understanding , nice person with whom you would love to work? Good! Give that item a 9 or a 10.

How do you feel about your job qualifications? Obviously somebody in the company must think that you would be capable to do the job, otherwise you would not have this offer. But let's say that you would be in a management position. You have led teams before, and you are not afraid of trade unions. However, your lack of experience in contract negotiating makes you feel at least a bit apprehensive about this item. Maybe you give a +5 or +6 score.

So, how do you feel about that job?

Score	Issue	Comments/Actions
_____	*proposed location (country, job site)*	
_____	*business situation (new venture vs. established situation)*	
_____	*specific duties/goals/ responsibilities*	
_____	*overall qualifications required for this job*	
_____	*type of work (manager vs. operations vs. on-line etc)*	
_____	*amount of past work experience for this job*	
_____	*international experience*	
_____	*degree of interest in the job*	
_____	*anticipated stress level*	
_____	*boss/supervisor*	
_____	*type of career move (lateral, step up or down)*	
_____	*type of assignment (family moves vs. single or split assignment)*	
_____	*salary*	
_____	*perks and additional benefits*	
_____	*employment prospects upon return*	
_____	*SUBTOTAL: THE JOB (Range: -150 to +150 points)*	

II) Proposed Location: Overall Impression
Based on Your Information

Score each item with your first reaction. Try not to dwell on each score. As explained above, use the scale ranging from −10 to +10. Score a 0 if you are neutral on this item. Leave items blank that you cannot answer due to lack of information.

Examples: You love people of different cultures, and your natural reaction is to dive into community and social projects. Your research tells you that you will have minimum exposure to your hosts. This fact could draw a serious negative score from you.

However, in your comments/actions column you might note that on the compound where you will live chances are pretty good that you meet other expats from all parts of the world with whom you can work and socialize. Would this counterbalance your initial negative reaction?

The climate issue appears twice. Maybe you feel very positively about the overall tropical climate in your host country. You give it a +9. From your research you learned that, due to your health status, the climate scores negatively. Think about the skin cancer that you had removed or about the asthma condition that is aggravated by humidity. You give it a −4 in the health section. Which score weighs heavier with you? What actions can you take in order to work around your health risks?

So what did you find out about your host country and how do you feel about it?

Score	Issue	Comments/Actions

Geographic location: score your feelings about the location—specifically:

_____ *The country itself*

_____ *The site: city vs. rural*

_____ *The climate*

_____ *Language*

_____ *Choice of accommodation*

_____ *Living in a compound*

_____ *Ability to mix with locals*

_____ *Presence of other expats*

_____ *Infrastructure (industrialized vs. third world)*

_____ *Reliable electrical supply*

_____ *Reliable communications (phone, fax, internet access)*

_____ *Adequate public transportation*

Health

_____ *Temperature and humidity (climate)*

_____ *Altitude*

_____ *Pollution*

_____ *Overall hygiene*

_____ *Safety of foods*

_____ *Safety of water supply*

_____ *Pests (cockroaches, spiders, snakes, etc.)*

_____ *Native diseases*

_____ *Requirement for special immunizations*

_____ *Status of health facilities*

_____ *Availability of practitioners, doctors, specialists*

_____ *Availability of pharmaceuticals*

_____ *Resources for "special needs"*

_____ *SUBTOTAL: LOCATION (Range: –250 to +250 points)*

III) Family Matters: How Do You Feel That the Following Issues Will Impact Your Chances of Becoming an Expat?

Score each item with your first reaction. Try not to think about the score. Use a scale of +10 to −10. Score a 0 if you are neutral on that item. Leave items blank that you cannot answer due to lack of information.

This is one of the most serious areas to explore. Don't let a low score discourage you immediately. All expat candidates face some serious conflicts involving family and property matters that could threaten the overseas assignment. You might have to do a bit of creative thinking in order to work around some of these roadblocks.

Examples: You have a child with emotional problems. You know from doing your homework that psychologists, counselors and other specialists are not available for help in your area. Besides, a move might aggravate the situation. You will probably feel that this item has a negative impact on your expat prospects. You might be convinced to give the item a −7 score, maybe less depending on the severity of the problem.

Your family depends on the spouse's income in order to make ends meet. For an overseas move heavy financial dependence on spouse income is in most cases a definite drawback. If your research also shows that the spouse will not be able to work overseas, you have two very negative scores against you.

However, if the family is not dependent on the spouse's income for sheer survival, score that item with a significant positive value in your favor.

So what does your research or even your intuition tell you about your ability to manage some of the following key family matters long distance or even on-site?

The bigger the problem, the lower the value that you assign.

Score	Issue	Comments/Actions
_____	Family financial dependence on spouse income	
_____	Opportunity for the spouse to work for pay overseas	
_____	Spouse emotional dependence on job/career	
_____	Opportunities for spouse activities overseas	
_____	Administration of family business	
_____	Investment management	
_____	Management of rental or speculative properties	
_____	Family home	
_____	Cars/boat	

Children

_____	Emotional state	
_____	Age issues (children are too young or are teenagers)	
_____	Special needs	

Other Family Issues

_____	Health problems	
_____	Aging parents in need of care	
_____	Pets	
_____	SUBTOTAL: FAMILY MATTERS (Range: −150 to +150 points)	

IV) The Society in Your Host Country

Score each item with your first reaction. Try not to think about the score. Use a scale of +10 to −10. Score a 0 if you are neutral on this item. Leave items blank that you cannot answer due to lack of information.

Examples: Your research tells you that your country has a stable government. There are no military coups in the making. This should make you feel wonderful. You give that place a +9. If you find that you will not be exposed to terrorist threats, that crime is not out of control and so on, feel good about that. Score those items with a positive value in your favor.

As you did your homework, what did you find out about the society in your host country? Was your confidence boosted, or were your worse fears confirmed? How do you feel about the following items? The less confident you are, the lower the score.

Score	Issue	Comments/Actions

Personal Safety
____ *Political situation (stable government vs. unrest)*
____ *Religious tensions*
____ *Terrorist threats*
____ *Violent crime*
____ *Property crime (break-ins, car theft etc)*
____ *Crime against foreigners*
____ *Safety for women and children*
____ *Freedom of movement for family (tied to a compound, travel limits)*

Acceptance of foreigners of your
____ *Nationality*
____ *Ethnic background*
____ *Religion*

Status of women
____ *Gender discrimination and equal rights*
____ *Requirement for special dress*
____ *Freedom of movement for women*
____ *Degree of chauvinism*
____ *SUBTOTAL: THE SOCIETY (Range: -150 to + 150 points)*

V) Education: Based on Your Information How Do You Feel about the Education System in Your Host Country?

Score each item with your first reaction. Try not to dwell on each score. Use a scale from –10 to +10. Score a 0 if you are neutral on that item. Leave items blank that you cannot answer due to lack of information.

Examples: When we went on assignment, the local public school did not excite me at all. I gave it a –6. The private school with its tougher curriculum scored a + 5. We sent our daughter to the private school. The fact that the company paid the tuition rated a +10 with me.

Score	Issue	Comments/Actions

Schools (availability and quality of education)

_____ *Language barrier (in what language are classes taught?)*

_____ *Public*

_____ *Private*

_____ *Boarding*

_____ *U.S. accredited curriculum*

_____ *Cost of tuition*

_____ *Requirement for uniforms*

_____ *Acceptable disciplinary rules*

_____ *Acceptable teaching style*

_____ *Availability of counseling services*

_____ *Availability of tutoring services*

_____ *Availability of transportation*

_____ *Ease of re-entry into U.S. school system after assignment*

_____ *Spouse/partner continuing education plans*

_____ *On-site opportunity for such education*

_____ *SUBTOTAL: EDUCATION (Range: –150 to + –150 points)*

VI) *Quality of life: In the End, How Important Do You Feel That the Following Items Are for Quality of Life?*
List of Wants and 'Must-haves'.

Think about the following items according to how important they are for your quality of life. You can replace my suggestions with your own preferences. Make sure that you have a total of 15 items in order to keep the scoring in balance.

Example: To you equal rights for both genders are very important for quality of life. They rate a +10.

Clear your mind and score each item according to your feelings. Try not to dwell on each score. Use a scale from −10 to +10. Score a 0 if you are neutral on that item. Leave items blank that you cannot answer due to lack of information. Do your scoring in pencil because there will be some corrections.

AFTER you have identified and rated your 'Must-Haves' for quality of life, think about with what your situation overseas will actually be like. You know what makes you happy, you know what will be offered. Weigh the facts! The result from this final analysis will give you the final scores for this exercise.

Examples: I told you in the book how my studies changed my mind rather drastically on small town living. I actually went from a negative to a positive value. The information that I gained vaporized some of my earlier biases. My thinking became a lot more flexible, to say the least.

Remember how you rated equal rights a +10? Your research tells you though that in your host country gender discrimination is rampant. As a matter of fact, women are second class citizens. Can you deal with this? Can you dull your senses for a while? Is the big adventure worth it? If the point is not negotiable, score it with a −10. Then again, you might decide that the experience is worth a compromise. Factor in your willingness to live with the situation and assign maybe a compromise +4.

Now for the final analysis: what have your studies taught you about your 'Must-Have' quality of life indicators? Adjust your scores.

Score	Issue	Comments/Actions
_____	City life	
_____	Specialty food items (organic, sugarfree, low fat etc)	
_____	Ethnic foods	
_____	Overall food safety	
_____	Restaurants	
_____	Personal safety	
_____	Personal freedom	
_____	Women's rights	
_____	Quality education	
_____	Shopping malls	
_____	Hobby stores	
_____	Movies	
_____	Plays	
_____	Music/ Opera	
_____	Sports	
_____	SUBTOTAL: QUALITY OF LIFE (Range: −150 to +150 points)	

Scoring Your Answers

After scoring the items on all pages, please remember to go back and look at all of the issues which you left blank. These are the areas where you need to get additional information. If you have more than a third of the items blank then you will have to fill in the blanks before you can proceed.

Now please circle all of the items which you gave a score of 0, –1, –2, –3, –4, –5, –6 –7, –8, –9 or –10. Then review these and think about possible solutions or actions that can be taken in order to alleviate problems: help from family, company, friends, boarding schools, compromises with employers on length or place of assignment, leave of absence for spouse etc. Record these in the 'Comments' space.

After you have completed this, then add the scores on each page and enter the number in the space provided. Then enter the subtotals below and add those to get your grand total.

____ SUBTOTAL: THE JOB
(possible score: +150 to –150)

____ SUBTOTAL: LOCATION
(possible score: +250 to –250)

____ SUBTOTAL: FAMILY MATTERS
(possible score: +150 to –150)

____ SUBTOTAL: THE SOCIETY
(possible score: +150 to –150)

____ SUBTOTAL: EDUCATION
(possible score: +150 to –150)

____ SUBTOTAL: QUALITY OF LIFE
(possible score: +150 to –150)

____ TOTAL
(possible score: +1000 to –1000)

Evaluating Your Scores:

+1000 to +700	This assignment looks very favorable for you
+700 to +300	This assignment looks favorable for you
+300 to −300	You probably need to address specific problems or you need to get much more information
−300 to −700	This assignment does NOT look favorable for you
−700 to −1000	Given your current circumstances, it is very unlikely that you will be happy with any expatriate assignment

The score itself is not critical. It is merely a guideline that is supposed to make you think. The more positively you feel about yourself, your family, the job and the host country the better the chance that you will all ride the wave of expat life happily together. In the end, YOU must decide whether you are even remotely willing to consider the assignment.

Test Your Motives

Instructions
1) Read through the seven common motives for going on an expatriate assignment. Can you think of any personal, additional items that might convince you to become an expat? If so, write those on the blanks: 8), 9) and 10).

2) Now go through the list and evaluate your feelings on each motive. Put them in ascending order of importance. 1 is the strongest motive you have. It really inspires you. 10 (or 7 if you did not write in any ideas of your own) is the weakest motive.

Our top three ratings were: personal desire for a change, timing and travel. We had no guarantees on the career move, and financial incentives of any kind by themselves would not have convinced me to put myself through the change and turmoil.
So, what makes you tick?

Motive Rating:
(I am interested in this expatriate assignment because:)
_____ 1) *Personal desire for a change/adventure*
_____ 2) *Timing of offer is right for expat/for family*
_____ 3) *Positive career move*
_____ 4) *Travel opportunities*
_____ 5) *Financial incentives*
_____ 6) *No option but to accept!*
        (my partner's current job is in jeopardy)
_____ 7) *Getting away from it all!*
_____ 8) *Other Reason* _____
_____ 9) *Other Reason* _____
_____ 10) *Other Reason* _____

As you check your ratings, make sure that your motives are strong enough to carry you through the length of your assignment. Are your hopes and dreams backed by facts?

If you rated the money incentives very highly, make sure that the company's offer really meets your expectations.

If you feel very strongly that you have no options or that the assignment is an opportunity to escape personal problems, you need help.

Questions to Ask the Employer

Before you agree to relocation, get some resolution on details that have been known to cause a lot of aggravation for expats.

Pay (also see Personal Finances – Worksheets)

_____ *a)* *split between accounts*
_____ *b)* *into one account only*
_____ *c)* *frequency of pay*
_____ *d)* *in line with overseas cost of living*
_____ *e)* *details on incentives/perks*
_____ *f)* *compensation for loss of spouse's income*
_____ *g)* *company assistance to help spouse find work overseas*

Tax Issues

_____ *a)* *name of tax consultant*
_____ *b)* *details on time deadlines*
_____ *c)* *details on filing procedure*
_____ *d)* *details on deductions*
_____ *e)* *details on documents to save*
_____ *f)* *overseas property ownership/investments*
_____ *g)* *who pays penalties for errors/late fees*

Immigration

_____ *a)* *clarify exact status*
_____ *b)* *visa rights and limitations*
_____ *c)* *spouse employment options*

Details on personal budget

_____ *a)* *housing allowance*
_____ *b)* *furniture allowance*
_____ *c)* *transportation allowance*
_____ *d)* *relocation allowance*
_____ *e)* *repatriation allowance*

_____ *f)* *help with financial management*
_____ *g)* *school tuition for children*
_____ *h)* *long distance phone allowance*

Health insurance
_____ *a)* *local on-site policy: name & details of coverage*
_____ *b)* *insured through home-based policy*
_____ *c)* *instructions on claim filing*
_____ *d)* *person in charge of health benefits*
_____ *e)* *"special needs" covered*
_____ *f)* *pregnancy covered*
_____ *g)* *ambulance services covered*
_____ *h)* *counseling coverage*
_____ *i)* *dental/eye needs covered*
_____ *j)* *special clinic or doctors for expats*
_____ *k)* *emergency assistance program (SOS)*
_____ *l)* *24 hour emergency number at home office*

Property issues
If you keep your house:
_____ *a)* *who manages property/name of person in charge*
_____ *b)* *list of 'management' services*
_____ *c)* *who keeps rent money*
_____ *d)* *reports on property status*
_____ *e)* *who pays increase in fees for insurance & property*
taxes

Property storage issues
_____ *a)* *name of company*
_____ *b)* *name of contact person*
_____ *c)* *limits on amount stored*
_____ *d)* *exception items*
_____ *e)* *insurance of goods*
_____ *f)* *penalties for early removal*
_____ *g)* *accessibility of goods*

Moving issues

_____ a) *allowed shipping weight*
_____ b) *excluded items (car, piano, etc.)*
_____ c) *amount of air freight*
_____ d) *amount of surface freight*
_____ e) *insurance details*

Transportation overseas

_____ a) *lease, rental or personal car*
_____ b) *clarify insurance details if you drive (liability, collision, personal injury)*
_____ c) *drivers' license requirements*
_____ d) *clarify insurance if local driver is hired*
_____ e) *clarify supplemental credit card insurance issues*
_____ f) *rental car insurance for home leave or trips*

Travel allowance for family

_____ a) *fixed amount to be used at leisure*
_____ b) *home visits paid for only*
_____ c) *emergency home visits covered*

Job security for expat upon repatriation

_____ a) *does employer have policy regarding returning expatriates?*
_____ b) *what is the employer's record with regard to returning expatriates?*
_____ c) *what are your partner's plans long term, to stay with employer or leave?*

Health Checklists

Medical Needs & Documents:
EVERY family member needs:

____   *General medical check-up*
____   *Visit to specialist if applicable*
____   *Dental visit*
____   *Eye exam if applicable*
____   *Immunizations / boosters*
____   *Up-to-date immunization record*
____   *Spare pair of prescription glasses/contact lenses*
____   *Enough contact lens care products*
         (difficult to find items)
____   *Pair of UV protectant sunglasses*
____   *Sunscreen for skin type*
____   *Allergy-Alert identification if applicable*
____   *Blood type information*
____   *Prescriptions filled*
____   *Summary of health history from doctor*
____   *Copies of prescriptions: medications*
____   *Copies of prescriptions: glasses*
____   *Copies of special tests: Ultrasound*
____   *Electrocardiogram (ECG or EKG)*
____   *Scans*
____   *Hearing tests*

Self-Treatment Medications:
Check with the doctor or pharmacist on items for

____   *Cold/Sinus medicine (talk about Zinc lozenges*
         and Echinacea!)
____   *Throat lozenges*
____   *Flu medicine*
____   *Travelers diarrhea*
____   *Electrolyte replacement*
____   *Stomach acid reducers/antacids*

_____ *Laxatives*
_____ *Rash/itch creams*
_____ *Allergy medication*
_____ *Minor pain relievers*
_____ *Sleep aids*
_____ *Vitamin/mineral supplements*
_____ *Antibiotics if applicable*
_____ *Telephone numbers of your physicians*
_____ *Telephone numbers of your pharmacist*
_____ *Have all written material (summaries, test reports) translated into the language and alphabet of your host country*

Emergency Kit:
Discuss the contents with your doctor or pharmacist
_____ *Box with Band-Aids of various sizes*
_____ *Bandage rolls, narrow and medium width*
_____ *Adhesive, non-stick bandage pads*
_____ *Gauze pads, different sizes for cleaning and light bandaging*
_____ *Hypoallergenic bandage tape*
_____ *Box with various size net-style sleeves (hold bandages in place)*
_____ *Ace bandages 3" size (for sprains or snake bite pressure bandage)*
_____ *Pre-moistened skin wipes or antiseptic solution in plastic bottle*
_____ *Antibiotic/antiseptic cream*
_____ *Cream for treating minor burns (ask MD)*
_____ *Saline Solution for cleansing wounds (I carried a plastic bottle of saline nasal spray destined for on the spot wound care.)*
_____ *Eye wash solution*
_____ *Package of Kleenex*
_____ *Tweezers*

_____ *Scissors*
_____ *Safety pins*
_____ *Fever thermometer*
_____ *First Aid instruction cards (how to treat burn, snake bite, how to do CPR.)*
_____ *Package with emergency blanket*

If you relocate in country with unreliable hygiene standards:
_____ *Some syringes: 1cc, 3cc and 5cc sizes are usually most practical*
_____ *Needles for intramuscular (IM) and subcutaneous use (subq)*
_____ *Water purification tablets*

Note: If the company provides you with a ready-made kit, make sure that it is complete, that you know what everything is for and how to use it.

Moving Checklist

What do you take? What do you leave behind? Where do you leave it? Separate the inventory into 4 sections: Storage, sell/give away, safekeeping, take along.

Here are some broad guidelines:

Put in Storage:
_____ *Furniture*
_____ *carpets, rugs*
_____ *heavy exercise equipment (home gyms, treadmills etc)*
_____ *electrical appliances, unless useable on site*
_____ *electronic equipment unless useable on site*
_____ *good china and glassware*
_____ *extra cutlery*
_____ *antiques*
_____ *art work, sculpture*

_____ *extra books*
_____ *magazine collections*
_____ *hobby equipment unless light and easily movable*
_____ *gardening appliances*
_____ *the barbecue*
_____ *tools, especially power tools*
_____ *car and motorcycles if accepted by company*

Note: Some articles might be refused by the storage company such as pianos, guns, ammunition or extremely valuable art work antiques, china, silver etc. You might have to make your own arrangements by appealing to family and friends.

Sell/Give Away (Items that are not worth storing or taking):
_____ *Extra clothes*
_____ *extra books*
_____ *excess music tapes and CDs*
_____ *obsolete toys*
_____ *car*
_____ *motorcycle*
_____ *bicycles*
_____ *old appliances, stereos, furniture, rugs, drapes etc.*
_____ *plants*
_____ *pets*

Put in Safe (Keep in safety deposit box at bank or in attorney's office):
Some people take all of their important papers with them on assignment. Others carry copies and register a trusted family member, usually the one who has the power of attorney, with the bank so that this person has access to the safety deposit in case of need.
_____ *Originals of property deeds*
_____ *car titles*
_____ *insurance policies*

_____ *will*
_____ *power of attorney*
_____ *investment papers*
_____ *sale documents of house*
_____ *sale documents of cars*
_____ *rental property leases*
_____ *tax files*
_____ *birth certificates*
_____ *marriage license*
_____ *unneeded credit cards*
_____ *family pictures and slides*
_____ *jewelry, heirlooms*

Take Along:
_____ *Clothing, colors and styles compatible with new home*
_____ *some toys and games for kids*
_____ *some books*
_____ *select electric appliances if useable overseas*
_____ *kitchen equipment: pots, pans, trays, utensils*
_____ *everyday china*
_____ *everyday glassware*
_____ *everyday cutlery*
_____ *favorite piece of furniture for that down-home feeling*
_____ *one album with photos of family and friends*
_____ *some pictures or posters that connect you to your home*
_____ *selection of hand tools, (hammer, screwdriver etc.)*
_____ *hobby equipment if compact*
_____ *sports equipment if compact and absolutely necessary*
_____ *a selection of music tapes and CDs*
_____ *walkman/Discman*

Change of Address Checklist

_____ *Post Office*
_____ *Family members*
_____ *Friends*
_____ *Neighbors*
_____ *Business partners/associates*
_____ *Church*
_____ *Tenants if you rent out property*
_____ *Landlord if you are a renter*
_____ *Spouse's employer*
_____ *Children's schools*
_____ *Clubs: business*
_____ *Clubs: social*
_____ *Clubs: book*
_____ *Clubs: athletic*
_____ *Professional licensing Board*
_____ *Tax office: State*
_____ *Federal*
_____ *Veterans' Administration if applicable*
_____ *Subscription services: newspapers*
_____ *newsletters*
_____ *magazines*
_____ *catalogues*
_____ *Banks*
_____ *Credit Union*
_____ *Financial consultants*
_____ *Brokers*
_____ *Credit card companies*
_____ *Visa*
_____ *MasterCard*
_____ *American Express*
_____ *Discover*

_____ *Diners Club*
_____ *Department stores*
　　　 other: _____

_____

_____ *Doctors: Family physician*
_____ *Pediatrician*
_____ *Dentist*
_____ *Specialists: dermatologist (skin)*
_____ *ophthalmologist (eyes)*
_____ *cardiologist (heart)*
_____ *psychologist*
　　　 other: _____

_____

_____ *Pharmacy*
_____ *Attorney*
_____ *Insurance companies: Property*
_____ *Automobile*
_____ *Life*
_____ *Health plan*
_____ *Property services:*
_____ *Telephone (local and long distance)*
_____ *Gas*
_____ *Electric*
_____ *Water*
_____ *Heating fuel*
_____ *Garbage*
_____ *Lawn and garden care*
_____ *Appliance maintenance contract*
_____ *Window washing service*
_____ *Cleaning service*
　　　 other: _____

_____

_____

_____

Last Minute Checklist

Check your travel documents
_____ a) passports and visas
_____ b) tickets
_____ c) travel itinerary

Did you
_____ a) mail the change of address cards
_____ b) notify the utilities of your move (for more help see "Notify of move/Address Change" Checklist)
_____ c) meet with the property manager
_____ d) make a will
_____ e) give power of attorney to anyone
_____ f) get the school transcripts
_____ g) have all prescriptions filled
_____ h) pick up health documents
_____ i) get sunglasses for all
_____ j) make copies of important documents that you need to take along
_____ k) pack some US checks for paying bills while overseas
_____ l) buy special treats and hard-to-get items

Did you put in safekeeping
_____ a) jewelry
_____ b) heirlooms
_____ c) unneeded credit cards
_____ d) originals of important papers (deeds, insurance policies etc)
_____ e) extra checks

Who
_____ a) knows where will is kept
_____ b) has access to safety deposit box

Repatriation Checklist

As soon as you know the date of your departure, start preparing for your move back to the homeland. Scan the "moving checklist" once more for help. Separate what you will ship from what you plan to sell or give away.

Consult the checklist on "Notification of change of address/move" for help. In addition, notify of your return

____ *Home office*
____ *a) supervisor*
____ *b) human resources*
____ *c) expat liaison*
____ *Storage company*
____ *Property manager to*
____ *a) assure timely departure of renters*
____ *b) give final status report on property*
____ *c) arrange any needed repairs*
____ *d) arrange cleaning of premises*
____ *e) provide a list of contractors that have worked on property during your absence*
____ *Tax consultant, to advise you on need for*
____ *a) bank documents from transfer or closure of accounts*
____ *b) statements from overseas internal revenue service*
____ *c) statements from immigration services*
____ *d) any special documents to be obtained before departure*

Before leaving obtain
____ *a) certificate for volunteer work performed*
____ *b) final job performance review*
____ *c) school transcripts for children*
____ *d) copies of any health services provided overseas. (prescriptions, glasses, X-rays, health history etc.)*

Bibliography

Reyer A. Swaak
Today's Expatriate Family: Dual Careers and Other Obstacles (includes reference for Windham International/NFTC Global Relocation Trends Survey 1994 Report)
Compensation & Benefits Review, American Management Association, 1995

Windham International/NFTC 1992
Expatriate Dual Career Survey Report

Expatriate Assignments May Not Be Fulfilling Their Objectives
Survey PERSONNEL JOURNAL, June 1996

John R. Engen
Coming Home
TRAINING magazine, March 1995

Joyce Sautters Osland
Working Abroad: a Hero's Adventure
Training & Development, November 1995

Linda Grant
That Overseas Job Could Derail Your Career
FORTUNE April 14, 1997

Larry Jenkins
Overseas Assignments: Sending The Right People
International HR Journal, Summer 1995 Vol. 4 / NO. 2

Mike Shoup, Newhouse News Service
Traffic danger is a major risk for American travelers abroad
Minneapolis STAR TRIBUNE, December 29 1996

J. Stewart Black, Hal B. Gregersen & Mark E. Mendenhall
Global Assignments
1992 Jossey-Bass Publishers, San Francisco

Diana Fairechild
JET SMART
1992 Flyana Rhyme Inc., Hawaii

International Travel and Health
1996 WHO
World Health Organization, United Nations

The MERCK MANUAL of Diagnosis and Therapy
Sixteenth Edition 1992
MERCK Research Laboratories
MERCK & CO Inc. Rahway, N.J.

Jane Brody
Hepatitis C looms as a silent threat to health.
Minneapolis STAR TRIBUNE, 26 January 1997

Katherine Griffin
The Time of Cholera.
HEALTH magazine, May/June 1993

US Pharmacist magazine
Health Gazette Medical News: Hint for Travelers Abroad
August 1992

Sudip Mazumdar
Flight From a Killer Bug.
NEWSWEEK, November 1996

AHFS DRUG INFORMATION
American Hospital Formulary Service 1995
American Society of Health-System Pharmacists
Bethesda, MD

Larry King
How to Talk to Anyone, Anytime, Anywhere
1995 Crown Trade Paperbacks, New York

Dale Carnegie
THE QUICK AND EASY WAY TO EFFECTIVE SPEAKING
1962 Pocket Books, Simon & Schuster, New York

Nathaniel Branden
THE POWER OF SELF-ESTEEM
1992 Health Communications Inc.
Deerfield Beach, Florida

Dr. Wayne W. Dyer
YOUR ERRONEOUS ZONES
1977 Avon Books, New York

Dr. Robert Anthony
THE ULTIMATE SECRETS OF TOTAL SELF-CONFIDENCE
1984 Berkley Books, New York

Index